With Love
from
Stephen

YOU ARE THE LIGHT OF THE WORLD

A UNIVERSAL 21st CENTURY MEDITATION COURSE

For Busy People
In 9 Simple Steps

BY STEPHEN WEBSTER

Published by Light Holistics Publications
7 Woodhouse Close, Warrington, Cheshire, WA3 6QP
www.lightholistics.com

Printed by the MPG Books Group
in the UK

ISBN 13 978-0-9560556-0-6

First Published in the UK December 2008

**LIGHT HOLISTICS
PUBLICATIONS**

ACKNOWLEDGEMENTS

On our journey through life we meet many people, all of whom teach us something. No ideas are entirely new. Insight is often handed down. All of the understandings and practices in this book are the result of such meetings, some of which were very close, and over long periods of time, while others were at a distance, and in a moment only. Some have been in body and some in spirit only. It may seem strange to acknowledge archetypal beings, along with people we have actually met in the flesh, but on the inner path the distinction is not significant. Everyone and everything flows into each other. Thank you to those beings, and anyone I've ever met, whose spirit has been a light to me on my journey!

My mother and father, Jesus Christ, Peter, Jim, Liz, George Fox, Buddha, Mr Meteyard, Mahatma Gandhi, Judith, Ram, Martin Luther King, Fuji Guruji, Mansukh Patel, Krishna, St Francis, Father Bede Griffiths, Marjory Sykes, Sathya Sai Baba, Yogananda, Siva, Maha Mai, Richard Everest, Francois, Atul, My Guardian Angel, Sister Rita, St Therese of Lisieux, Brother Roger, Sister Bozena, Miriam - The Little Arab, the Holy Spirit, Sri Ramana Maharshi, Ramakrishna, Gita, Shin Yu, Satyananda Saraswati, Padre Pio, St Ignatius, Father McManus, Usui, Mother Mary, Shirdi Baba, Hazrat Inayat Khan, John, Pir Vilayat Khan, Amma, Atum O Kane, Lily, Pir Zia, Aftab, Llewellyn Vaughan-Lee, Saki, Muhammed, Saj, Rasmik, Father Tony Slingo, Sivananda, Lesley Jones, Vicki, Ella, Paul, Julian, Thich Nhat Hanh, Pope Benedict, Arthur Weinberg.

A SPECIAL THANKS

Special thanks to Saj, Arthur Weinberg, my mother, Vicky, Michael Haighburgen, and James for help with proof-reading and suggestions for the book. Thanks very much to John, for last minute help with photographs.

CONTENTS

ILLUSTRATIONS

INTRODUCTION

This meditation course is designed for busy people in the 21st Century. It is ideal for people new to meditation, who may want an overview before committing themselves to one path or another. It is ideal for Yoga teachers, who want to explore more deeply the meditation aspects of their science. It is ideal for experienced meditators, who want to clarify and refine their practice. It is also ideal for people who want to discover who they are, or to change into the person they would like to be.

The language I use is simple, concise, practical and inspirational. It is the distilled wisdom of over 20 years travelling on the spiritual path, on a journey involving the world's largest spiritual traditions. The nine stages of meditation are a new way of presenting the inner journey, although nothing in the journey is actually new. The path is well-trodden. The only novelty is the need for universality and simplicity on our busy and ever-shrinking planet. I include quotes from major world scriptures and inspiring works at each meditation stage, to show you that this journey is ancient and profound, as well as simple and accessible to all. There are no secrets in spirituality. The only secret is the actual experience, which protects itself, by revealing itself, only to those who actually go through the process, passing each stage as they go.

This course is about practice. It is a manual for self-transformation. I recommend that you practise each of the meditations, one after the other. There is a progression in the meditations. At the same time, each meditation stands on its own. I expect you to find some of the practices work for you and others may not. This course is a tool for your empowerment. Use it to enlighten and inspire your journey. I explain the most profound spiritual teachings in the simplest language I can.

This book is an offering of peace. It is not designed as an alternative to any one authentic spiritual tradition. It is like a peace conference, where we celebrate the communality in all the worlds' traditions. It is the experience of most travellers on the path, that at some point, we will make a commitment to one core tradition. This course is designed to help you with that process. At the same time our times call for an increased recognition of our shared inheritance and destiny on planet earth, as there is something new and exciting about the way communications have brought us closer together. It is time for broad hearted, spiritual people to stand together and affirm an alternative to pure materialism.

I start by listing various definitions and benefits of meditation. We then work through each of the 9 stages, with a simple reflection, inspiration from the greatest world teachers, and 36 linked meditations. The power of this work is in the combination of structure and free flow. There is a real progression in meditation that you can measure using the scientific language of Yoga. At the same time each meditation is art - a free flowing experience in itself, which reaches beyond measurement into the heart.

Good luck on your journey! May you find happiness and the causes of happiness! May you find love and the causes of love! May you find beauty and the causes of beauty!

PART 1
WHAT IS MEDITATION?

The tomb of Hazrat Inayat Khan in Delhi, the bringer of a Universal form of Sufism to the West.

Like a multi-faceted diamond, meditation has many aspects and goes by many names. Reflect on each of the short descriptions overleaf. See which aspects resonate with you and which have something new to reveal to you.

MEDITATION HAS MANY ASPECTS

Peace of mind

Remembering who I am

Realising I am a child of god

Becoming one with the Creator

Self Realisation

Living from the heart

Mind, body and soul united

Love, truth and peace

Living in the eternal now

Practising the presence of God

Seeing the wood for the trees

Living in love and light

Living in the Sacred

Where suffering and bliss meet

Realising the Kingdom of Heaven within
Working for the Kingdom of Heaven without

The magnificent joy of being

God beyond and God within

A wave rising up from the ocean

Stepping off the wheel and helping the wheel move forward

World in the mind, mind in the heart

Perfect balance

Love, lover and beloved as one

See-er, seen and seeing as one

Realising the wholeness in the brokenness of life

Ordinary BECOMES extra-ordinary

Peace beyond understanding

PART 2
WHY MEDITATE?

Sivananda Yoga students from many lands meditating by the sea in Lithuania.

An elderly gentleman, a complete stranger, sitting on a wall in an Ashram (spiritual centre) in India, once opened up communication with me, as if we were old friends, by getting straight to the point. "Why is it, he asked rhetorically, that people embark on the spiritual path? Is it because they have experienced a great ecstasy and want the same experience again? Is it because they have suffered a great tragedy and desperately need peace? Or is it simply the spirit of enquiry that leads them on?

MEDITATION HAS MANY BENEFITS

RELEASING DEEP TENSIONS, WE CAN SELF-HEAL

WE CAN OVERCOME INHIBITIONS AND INNER BLOCKAGES

WE CAN STILL OUR INNER CHATTER

WE CAN BECOME MORE OPEN AND RESPONSIVE TO OTHERS

WE CAN DEVELOP GREATER SELF CONFIDENCE

WE CAN DISCOVER OUR NATURAL RHYTHM

WE CAN NURTURE OURSELVES AND OTHERS MORE

WE CAN LEARN TO RETURN LOVE FOR HATRED

WE CAN BECOME PART OF THE SOLUTION

WE CAN DISCOVER OUR PURPOSE IN LIFE

WE CAN DISCOVER HAPPINESS AND ITS CAUSES

WE CAN FIND INNER UNITY AND CREATE OUTER UNITY

WE CAN LEARN THE WAY OF THE HEART

WE CAN FALL IN LOVE WITH OURSELVES, CREATION AND THE CREATOR

WE CAN BECOME CENTRED IN THE SOURCE

WE CAN AWAKEN OUR INTUITIVE AND INSTINCTIVE CENTRES

WE CAN BECOME MORE SPONTANEOUS AND FREE

WE CAN BECOME MORE AWARE, AWAKE AND ALIVE.

WE CAN LEARN TO ENDURE AND OVERCOME

WE CAN FEEL MORE THE RICH TEXTURES OF LIFE

WE CAN OVERCOME OUR FEAR OF DEATH

WE CAN LEARN TO EMBRACE THE PRESENT MOMENT

WE CAN DEVELOP GREAT POISE, DIGNITY AND BALANCE

WE CAN LEARN TO READ THE BOOK OF LIFE ON MANY LEVELS

WE CAN EXPERIENCE PEACE BEYOND UNDERSTANDING

PART 3
THE NINE UNIVERSAL STAGES
OF MEDITATION

Shiva temple in Tiruvannamalai India. According to tradition, Shiva revealed the self transforming science of Yoga.

When we decide to meditate, when we commit ourselves to a 'spiritual path', we are really taking personal responsibility for our one-to-one relationship with the universe. We take a creative step, away from the protection of the crowd and automatic living, and we learn to face our Creator, our real Self. We may think it is 'our' decision. But really it is a calling, a vocation. The 'Way' has already been prepared for us. Our offerings of love become revelations of how much we are already loved. We are responding to an invitation to Loves' Banquet.

EVERY MEDITATION TRADITION CONTAINS ALL, OR SOME, OF THESE STAGES:

1. WITHDRAW

2. ASSUME MEDITATION POSTURE

3. BREATH AWARENESS

4. ATTUNE TO YOUR HEART CENTRE

5. FOCUS ON LIGHT

6. FOCUS ON SOUND

7. FOCUS ON PRESENCE

8. BORN AGAIN

9. LOVE AND SERVICE

STAGE 1

REVERSING THE CURRENT WITHDRAW

Beautifully adorned Buddha at Shrine to the Bodhi tree in Shri Lanka.

YOGIC WORD – PRATYAHARA

There is a Sufi tradition, that if you want to live a spiritual life in the world, you need to retreat for one hour per day, one day per week, one weekend per month, one month per year and one year in a lifetime. Regular practise is essential to feel the transforming effect of meditation.

CREATING THE RETREAT HABIT

Reversing the current of our awareness from its usual outward focus requires effort, commitment and even struggle. We need to create a meditation habit that develops as much momentum as the demands of outer life. Following these suggestions will help:

Time – Morning and evening, around sunrise and sunset, before breakfast and before dinner (after washing is ideal).

Duration – At least 20 minutes, twice per day is best. Once a day, once a week or even once a month, is better than nothing.

Space for meditation. Create a place set apart – a sacred space. Use incense, candles and uplifting images. Keep it clean and tidy.

Clothing - Loose, easy, natural fibre for good circulation. Wearing a shawl, kept just for meditation, can help trigger the retreat feeling.

Rhythm - keep it regular. Train the Subconscious mind/body - it will become conditioned to the habit and start to create a meditation presence on time. Make an appointment with the Angels and Masters of the Superconscious mind, and they will assist your efforts. Harmonise with family and friends, by letting them get used to your meditation habit.

Attitude – Let go of the past and the future. Get into a playful, childlike, holiday mood. Hand over responsibility for a moment.

Invoke Assistance – Call upon any inner Patrons, Masters, or Saviours you have faith in, to protect you on your journey across the dark sky of your subconscious mind, just as the stars light up the night sky. The pathway gets narrow in places and you may need a being of light to hold your hand. Seek the protection and inspiration of a faith, teacher or community, if it helps, remembering that no-one can give you Realisation and no-one can take it away from you.

Develop a core practise – If you dig one well, you can go deeper, quicker, than if you try to dig too many. Don't change your practise until it has reached its fulfilment. However many practises you study, keep a heart practise that can become the touchstone of your many changing moods and experiences. Allow your steadfastness in one method to polish your soul and overcome your inner demons.

Always learn about new methods and refine and revise your practice, staying open and free flowing, letting the heart be the guide. Stay fresh and inspired. Allow your practice to evolve with integrity. Learn from all, to distinguish the eternal from the temporary and purely cultural.

16

JESUS

'Seek first his kingdom and his righteousness, and all these things shall be yours as well. Therefore do not be anxious about tomorrow, for tomorrow will be anxious for itself.'

'First cleanse the inside of the cup and of the plate, that the outside also may be clean.'

'When you pray, go into your room and shut the door and pray to your Father who is in secret; and your Father who sees in secret will reward you.'

KRISHNA

'Let him find a place that is pure and a seat that is restful, neither too high nor too low, with sacred grass, and a skin and a cloth thereon.'

'Day after day, let the Yogi practise the harmony of the soul: in a secret place, in deep solitude, master of his mind, hoping for nothing, desiring nothing.'

PATANJALI

'Withdrawing the senses, mind and consciousness from contact with external objects, and then withdrawing them inwards towards the seer, is Pratyahara.'

RUMI

'The early breeze at dawn is the keeper of secrets. Don't go back to sleep! It is time for prayer, time to find what is your real need. Don't go back to sleep! The door of the One is open, always. Don't go back to sleep!'

BUDDHA

'Do not look for bad company, or live with men who do not care. Find friends who love the truth.'

'If you cannot Master yourself, the harm you do turns against you grievously.'

'Sit in the world, sit in the dark. Sit in meditation sit in light. Choose your seat. Let wisdom grow.'

SACRED INVOCATIONS

Every meditation tradition uses beautiful prayers to create the ideal mind-set for the spiritual journey and to appeal for assistance from sacred sources. Here are six classic examples from the inner adventure of humankind.

NATIVE AMERICAN INDIAN TRADITION

Song of the Sky Loom
Oh, our Mother the Earth;
Oh, our Father the Sky,
Your children are we,
With tired backs.
We bring you the gifts of love.
Then weave for us a garment of brightness...
May the warp be the white light of morning,
May the welt be the red light of evening,
May the fringes be the fallen rain,
May the border be the standing rainbow.
Thus weave for us a garment of brightness
That we may walk fittingly where birds sing;
That we may walk fittingly where the grass is green.
Oh, Our Mother Earth;
Oh, Our Father Sky.

HINDU TRADITION

O blazing light!
Awaken my heart
Awaken my soul
Ignite my darkness
Tear the veils of silence
And fill my temple with glory.

BUDDHIST TRADITION

May all sentient beings gain happiness
And the cause of happiness.
May all beings be free from suffering
And the cause of suffering.

CHRISTIAN TRADITION

Lord, make me an instrument of Thy peace!
Where there is hatred, let me sow love;
Where there is injury, pardon;
Where there is doubt, faith;
Where there is despair, hope;
Where there is darkness, light;
Where there is sadness, joy.
O Divine Master, grant that I may not
So much seek to be consoled, as to console;
To be understood, as to understand;
To be loved, as to love.
For it is in giving that we receive,
It is in pardoning that we are pardoned.
It is in dying that we are born to eternal life.

SUFI TRADITON

Toward the One
The Perfection of Love,
Harmony and Beauty,
The only Being
United with all the illuminated souls,
Who form the embodiment of the Master,
The Spirit of Guidance.

BAHAI TRADITION

O God! Refresh and gladden my spirit.
Purify my heart.
Illumine my powers.
I lay all my affairs in thy hand.
Thou art my Guide and my Refuge.
I will no longer be sorrowful and grieved;
I will be a happy and joyful being.
O God! I will no longer be full of anxiety,
nor will I let trouble harass me.
I will not dwell on the unpleasant things of life.
O God! Thou art more friend to me than I am to myself.
I dedicate myself to Thee, O Lord.

MEDITATION 1
IMAGES OF RETREAT

Sit silently. Slowly reflect on each image in turn. Feel how it touches you. Let the image sink into your subconscious, inducing the condition of retreat.

Time for me
Space and time
Alone with my thoughts
Alone with my feelings
Closing down the senses
Turning within, reversing my consciousness
Taking a moments pause
Taking a moment to breathe
Letting out a deep sigh
Letting go....loosening up
Becoming easy
Relaxing...resting
Going deep....going far out
Stepping through the inner door
Surfing the wave of feeling
Rising above it all
Seeing the wood for the trees
Stepping off the wheel
Stopping the world
Silence.....stillness
Presence, feeling, being
Listening to the still, small voice within
The voice of conscience
The language of the Heart
The song of love
The sound of sweet inspiration
Lighting the inner light
Fanning the inner flame
Dissolving in the light.....becoming the light
Remembering who I am
Remembering my Self.....the source
Finding God....the centre
The heart of love
All is well.

MEDITATION 2
USING THE SENSES TO RETREAT

Smell
Become aware of your sense of smell. What can you smell? What is your sense of smell experiencing, as you sit? What flavour does life have for you now? Do you have a good taste in your mouth?

Sight
Bring your attention to your sense of sight. Become aware of every detail that you can see, right here, right now. Imagine you are a new baby, seeing for the first time, and that you don't know what anything is. Without fixing your eye on any detail, take in the whole vista before you. Let your eyes be passive, as images flow into your eyes. Ask yourself 'on which side of these eyelids am 'I' on, inside or out? Do I know?' Become absorbed in the sensation of seeing and allow yourself to flow wherever it leads.

Sound
Close your eyes and travel within. Bring your awareness to your sense of hearing. Become aware of all the sounds you can hear - sounds close and far, in the foreground and background, continuous and intermittent. Now forget about details and concentrate on the whole symphony of sound. The movement and rhythm of the sound you are hearing. What is the sound of the sound? Become aware of sound as single phenomenon, without labels - the essence of the sound, within and without. Merge with sound.

Feeling
Move your attention to the sense of feeling. What sensations are you experiencing in your body? Feel the ground under your feet, the air on your skin, sensations in your body, feelings of heat and cold, hardness and softness, pain and pleasure. Now become aware of the sensation of your body, as a whole. What is the feeling of the whole 'you'? Does feeling travel beyond your body? Can you sense a presence in the room and beyond? Become aware of the centre of feeling, in your heart. Listen to your heart. Surf the wave of feeling.

Knowing
Drop your association with, and concentration on, your senses. Let go of all concentrations. Let go. What is left? Who am I? In the space between my thoughts where am I? Become the dew drop merging with the ocean. Allow yourself to emerge from the ocean as a wave. Ride that wave.

MEDITATION 3
FOCUSING ON ONE POINT

Sit still, with a straight spine and relaxed body. Become aware of your breathing. Every time you breathe in, breathe deeply into your solar plexus.

Bring your attention to the room you are sitting in. Notice everything - things you don't normally have time to notice. Become very present, awake, alert, sharp and alive. Shake your whole body a couple of times, just to make sure your energy and awareness is very vital. Look up, look down, to each side – don't miss anything.

Now steady your gaze. Stop moving your head. Just focus on the whole picture directly in front of you - the scene that meets your eyes. Now start to narrow and lower your focus. Focus on a point directly in front of you, probably on a wall. Imagine a line travelling from that point to you along the ground. Begin to follow that line backwards towards you. Trace it back to the floor, directly beneath you, maybe even to the tip of your nose. Don't strain your eyes, stay relaxed and simply focus on this point very close to you.

Your vision has narrowed down to a single point. You are no longer focused on the multiplicity of images, as you were before. Keeping your focus fixed on a single point, become aware of the presence of stillness, building up within you. When you can really feel that stillness, that presence, that inner reservoir of being, close your eyes and stay in that feeling as long as you can. As it says in the Bible, 'Be still, and know that I am God'.

STAGE 2

KING OR QUEEN ON A MAT
ASSUME MEDITATION POSTURE

A Buddhist friend sitting straight but relaxed in Kataragama Sri Lanka.

YOGIC WORD – ASANA

As you breathe in, feel your spine lengthen, extend and straighten upwards. Breathing out, feel your body and mind to be perfectly poised, balanced and at rest.

Body relaxed – Let go and feel soft and easy. **Spine straight** – aids energy flow, balances muscles and maintains alertness. **Straight neck** - Tuck your chin in and extend the back of your neck a little, to get the feeling, and then relax. **Long back** - Suck your abdomen in and lengthen your lower back a little, to get the feeling of a lifted lower spine, and then relax. **Arms and legs placed with purpose** – as per need.

LEG POSTURE – YOGIC WORD IS 'ASANA'
Cross legged – Centred - Usually Eastern tradition. Spine connects to earth, legs create closed circuit. I am in the centre, one with the One. My body is a miniature template of the universe. Develops peace, authenticity, height, depth, balance - God within.

Kneeling - Petitioning - Usually Western tradition-Prayerful. My Beloved completes me. I embrace and petition my Beloved. My body is half of the whole. Develops love, flow, responsiveness, breadth and openness - God without.

24

Sitting in Chair – Any feeling. Feet connect to Mother Earth. Head connects to Father in heaven. Heart in the middle. Universal. Hand position determines feeling.

HANDS – YOGIC WORD IS 'MUDRA'

Hands open and facing up - giving to, and receiving from, the environment. **Hands together** or palm down on knees – withdrawing from environment, building up inner energy – known as 'Prana' in India, 'Chi' in China or 'Spirit' in Western traditions.

5 HAND POSITION EXAMPLES

1. Hands in prayer position – left and right side balanced, wrists touching heart, finger tips touching heaven - heart reaching up.
2. Fingers interlocked–energy withdrawn and recirculating. Retreat.
3. Right hand on top of left – Concentration, Buddha/Siva position, union of higher and lower natures - **Bhairava Mudra** (fierce).
4. Fingers and thumbs interlocked, with index fingers touching, pointing forward –**Yoni (Womb)Mudra**. Opens elbows and heart.
5. Two hands separate palms up or down. Thumb and index fingers on each hand, touched together with other fingers straight – **Jnana Mudra**(Truth). Uniting the individual soul with Universal Being.

BUDDHA

'Beware of the anger of the body. Master the body. Let it serve the truth.'

'Like a broken gong, be still, be silent. Know the stillness of freedom where there is no more striving.'

'To straighten the crooked you must first do a harder thing – straighten yourself.'

'For the mind talks. But the body knows.'

KRISHNA

'With upright body, head and neck which rest still and move not.'

SVATMARAMA

'Asanas make one firm, free from maladies and light of limb.'

PATANJALI

'Asana is perfect firmness of body, steadiness of intelligence and benevolence of spirit.'

'Perfection in an Asana is achieved when the effort to perform it becomes effortless and the infinite being within is reached.'

ST PAUL TO THE CORINTHIANS

'Your body, you know, is the temple of the Holy Spirit, who is in you since you receive him from God. You are not your own property; you have been bought and paid for. That is why you should use your body for the glory of God.'

GENESIS

'So God created man in his own image, in the image of God he created him; male and female he created them.'

LAO TZU

'When people are born they are supple, and when they die they are stiff...thus stiffness is the companion of death, flexibility a companion of life.'

MEDITATION 4 (CENTRED POSTURE)
TRACING ENERGY UP YOUR SPINE

Sit with your spine very erect, placing your hands on your lap. As you breathe in, instead of thinking that the breath is travelling down into your lungs, imagine that the breath is travelling up your spine. According to the science of Yoga, this change in our normal way of thinking increases the subtle energy flow, and our sense of vitality, up and down the spine. As you breathe out, imagine that you are breathing down your spine. Breathe up and down your spine. As you breathe in, get the feeling of raising your energy up your spine and out the top of your skull into the Cosmos. As you breathe out, get the feeling that the breath of the Cosmos is descending down on your skull and travelling down your spine to earth. Become aware of the base of your spine connected to earth and the top of your skull connected to the sky, and you as a conduit in between. In India the creative, magnetic, 'feminine' energy connected with the earth, is called 'Sakti', and the formless, transcendent source from which energy descends, 'Siva'.

Reach your arms and hands out, palm down, feeling the magnetic connection between the palms of your hands and Mother Earth. Breathing in, draw your hands into the base of your spine and up the front of your body, fingers pointing inwards towards the spine, lifting the Sakti energy up. Passing your heart centre, rotate your hands inwards and palm upwards. Rising further, stretch your arms out and above your head - hands face upwards, as if gathering cosmic energy from Siva above.

As you breathe out, feel that energy descending through your hands and your spine. Retrace the journey of your arms and hands back down the spine, turning the fingers inwards, as they pass the heart centre, and downwards, tracing the energy down to your lap and back out to Mother Earth.

Continue this cycle as you breathe in and out. Feel the magnetic connection between your hands and spine and the magnetic energy travelling up and down the spine - up into the Cosmos and back down into the earth. You can intensify the feeling by visualizing your breath as light, travelling up and down your spine, connecting to the light in the starry skies and the electro-magnetism in Mother Earth. Now relax in your own space, and just be, feeling the effects of your energy revitalized and buoyant.

MEDITATION 5 (CENTRED POSTURE)
MY BODY IS A TEMPLE OF THE HOLY SPIRIT

Sit still, breathing deeply, feeling your head, heart and solar plexus centre. Meditate on the idea that your body is a temple of the Holy Spirit, a sacred structure, a Yantra, a Mandala, in itself, a sign and symbol of the Divine, as in the word 'Sacrament'. Simply sitting still, the structure of your body begins to generate a spiritual experience, as you become aware of subtle energy flows that you didn't notice before. In the yogic tradition, the centres through which these subtle energy currents funnel are called 'chakras' and 7 centres are usually highlighted to create an energy map of the body.

Become aware of the base of your spine, formed around the principle of being earthed, rooted and secure - 1st Chakra. Become aware of your reproductive centre, formed around the principle of dependence, relationships and creativity - 2nd Chakra. Become aware of your solar plexus, formed around the principle of depth, independence, peace, power and spiritual centredness - 3rd Chakra. Become aware of your heart centre, formed around the principle of interconnectedness and love flowing out through the hands - 4th Chakra. Become aware of your throat centre, formed around the principle of speech, communication and higher self expression - 5th Chakra. Become aware of your forehead and back of the head, formed around the principle of vision, wisdom and intuition - 6th Chakra. Become aware of the top of your head, formed around the principle of transcendence, surrender and connectivity to a higher universal consciousness - 7th Chakra.

Imagine that your body is already a perfect structure, formed, as the Bible says, in the image of God. Imagine the edge of your body as an ideal shape, generating a spiritual harmony that is rippling inwards and elevating your soul. Visualize and feel your soul shining, as your body becomes completely still, poised in perfect balance. Realise, that the template on which your body is designed is everlasting, passed on from generation to generation. Realise, as you sit in meditation, that through your body, you can connect to the design upon which your body is based, the genetic and etheric template that manifested your body. Connecting to the template that manifested your body, connect to the manifestor of all bodies, the creator of the first gene, the Father of the first Adam, the One before Many, the Source, Alpha and Omega.

MEDITATION 6 (CENTRED POSTURE)
MY BODY IS A YANTRA (SACRED GEOMETRY)

4 - RECTANGLE

Meditate on the shape of a rectangle. Feel yourself sitting in a rectangle. Feel how the shape of the square evokes feelings of security, protection, order, strength and being grounded. See how your legs make the shape of a rectangle when you sit cross legged, forming a firm foundation. If you are sitting in a chair, notice how we choose to sit in rectangular shapes.

3 - TRIANGLE

Now take a line away and meditate on the shape of a triangle. Imagine yourself sitting in a triangle. See how your body makes the shape of a triangle in the vertical dimension, especially when you sit to meditate, cross-legged. Feel the energy of movement within a protected area that the triangle creates. Feel the sensation of your energy rising upwards towards a point. Now visualize a downward triangle. Feel the sensation of energy descending down from above. Feel the piercing quality of the tip of the triangle and its capacity to move us to new dimensions.

2 - CROSS

Now take another line away and meditate on two lines. Cross them over each other and meditate on the image of a cross. See how your body forms a cross, between the horizontal dimension of your arms, reaching out to all, and the vertical dimension of your spine, reaching upwards to higher dimensions. Feel how two lines crossing create a friction, but also a perfect balance. Notice how your heart sits at the intersection between these two lines in your body. Balancing the needs of those around, with our personal aspirations, requires us to keep our heart centre open.

1 - CIRCLE

Now visualize a single line. The only way to draw a single, unbroken line, is a circle. Visualize yourself in a perfect circle. Feel how the circle seems to protect you, without the rigidity of the square. Attune to the feeling of wholeness and harmony without end - the feeling of eternity. Feel how the circle holds a feminine quality, which seems to nurture, while at the same time radiating like the sun, manifesting from the centre. Imagine the circle reduced to its smallest dimension, as a dot. Imagine travelling through that dot, in the core of your being, into new dimensions, not dreamed of.

MEDITATION 7 (PRAYER POSTURE)
THE 5 STAGES OF PRAYER

Gratitude - Hands in prayer position, become aware of all the blessings in your life, for which you can be grateful - everything you take for granted, every grace from the smallest to the greatest. Fill your heart with gratitude and feelings of warmth towards your creator and all those who have assisted you. Count your blessings. This practise can bring you great joy, anytime.

Contrition - Become aware of all the pain in your psyche - all the dashed dreams, all the suffering people have caused you, and you have caused others. Feel the wounds that you are carrying. Call to mind people whom you wish to forgive, and from whom you wish forgiveness. Imagine yourself embracing those people in mutual understanding, contrition and love. Meditation is like peeling an onion. It will open up deeper and deeper layers in our psyche, some of them painful. Rather than denying your pain, embrace your suffering with loving understanding, as a mother cradles a child.

Petition - Become aware of all the desires and wishes of your heart - all the unfulfilled needs and projects of your life. Feel yourself petitioning your Creator for assistance in your everyday and lifelong challenges. Lay all your burdens, hopes and dreams at the feet of your chosen image of perfection and feel the assistance of universal power, love and wisdom. Very often we reach an impasse in life. We can't see a way forward. Rather than considering our destiny to be random, we embrace and petition the unseen mystery with love, believing that the universe has a heart.

Love - Now we reach beyond petitioning, hopes and dreams to the present moment. We recall those moments of love in our life which made life worth living. We remember those experiences of beauty which lifted our hearts, for a moment, above the mundane and profane. Enter the realm of artists and mystics. All those experiences exist, right here, right now, in your heart. You can embrace heaven, right now, with your heart.

Knowledge - Love is about embracing the 'other'. Eventually the two become one. There is no other. As Jesus said, we become one with the Father. Love melts into union. So, letting go of all striving, stop running away from the sacred and beautiful work of divinity that you are, and just be.

MEDITATION 8 (PRAYER POSTURE)
BODY PRAYER FROM THE SUFI TRADITION

As children we are often familiar with the idea that God is in heaven, on a cloud in the sky. As we grow older, we realise that this isn't exactly true. And yet from a physiological and psychological point of view, it is partly true that God is in the sky. Our bodies are designed on the principle that wisdom is above, in the head, and waste materials are ejected below, at the bottom of the spine. Our feet walk on the planet very slowly, whilst our head can be in the clouds, dreaming dreams instantaneously, which can manifest later into great projects. When our life on earth comes to an end, our body returns to the earth, and our breath returns to the atmosphere. In a sense, we are a point of intersection, between the forces of the Cosmos, which appear to be above, and the massive reality that is our planet, which is below. In the middle, in a unique cross-section of time and space, is our heart, putting the dreams of heaven into practise, on the reality which is Mother Earth. It is only those with great heart, who see great projects through many trials to the end.

Kneeling in prayer position, if you can, or sitting in a chair, lift your hands up into the air and repeat the words, "You are my spirit". Become aware that you didn't create your spirit. It is a gift from above. Become aware of your transcendent dimension, your dimension in spirit, the idea of the Creator - the Father in heaven, the feeling of soul rather than body and the sense that we all came from one energy, point or seed.

Bringing your hands down to your knees, repeat the words "I am your body". Become aware that your body is a gift from Mother Earth. Become aware of your created dimension, your body, and how your body is a formation of the earth, eventually returning to the earth, just as the earth will one day be consumed by our sun.

Placing your hands on your heart, repeat the words "My Holy One". Become aware of yourself, as a unique intersection in time and space, between heaven and earth. Become aware of your heart, as the place in your body where the aspirations of heaven and the realities of earth meet, and where the need to reach out and the need to travel high and deep, come together. Feel your heart as the Kingdom of Heaven within, the goal and resting place of all the world's spiritual traditions, and at the same time the only place that is uniquely, and most preciously, you.

MEDITATION 9 (PRAYER POSTURE)
THE LORDS PRAYER

Place your body in prayer position. The essence of this meditation is to repeat the words of this famous prayer and pause for meditation and reflection at each stage. Here are some ideas for reflection.

Our Father who art in Heaven, Hallowed be Thy Name
Become aware of the transcendent dimension, the dimension of spirit, the feeling of Heaven Above, the space within and around everything, the idea of an intelligence behind all intelligences, a light behind all lights, a heart at the centre of the universe.

Thy Kingdom come, Thy will be done, on earth as it is in Heaven
Become aware of the created dimension in life. The needs and aspirations of people on earth, the potential to order life creatively or destructively, to create beautiful objects or ugly objects, to live relationships full of love or hatred. Become aware of the hard work and love we need to put our ideals and inspirations into practise.

Give us this day our daily bread
Become aware of all our material needs, and how we can relate these basic needs to our highest ideals, or instead lose sight of our highest aspirations, in the struggle simply to survive. In asking our creator to help with every detail of our life, our whole life becomes sacred.

Forgive us our trespasses as we forgive those who trespass against us
Realise how, what we get in life, is a reflection, in the long run, of what we give. Reflect on how, in embracing the brokenness of those around us, we are actually embracing ourselves.

And lead us not into temptation but deliver us from evil
Realise how, every second of the day, we choose our actions, plant the seeds of our destiny, and create the universe we live in. At the same time, realise how we rely on our Creator to inspire us.

For Thine is the Kingdom, the power and the glory, for ever and ever, Amen.
In the experience of blissful unity, the fruit of a beautiful life, we can experience euphoric and ecstatic moments without the need for alcohol, drugs, or stimulants. The greatest joy is already within.

STAGE 3

THE BREATH OF LIFE
AWARENESS OF BREATH

A staggeringly beautiful evening at St.Davids in Wales - fresh and expansive.

YOGIC WORD – PRANAYAMA

If you are struggling to meditate, you can try this: Sit comfortably, and focus your attention on your abdomen, expanding and contracting. Notice your breathing slowing down and deepening. Listen to the sound of the breath, flowing in and out of your nostrils, like the sea, ebbing and flowing. This deep abdominal breathing, practised every day, can transform your nervous system and your life.

BREATH AWARENESS LEADS US DEEPER INTO MEDITATION

Awareness of breath

There is a vital link between our breath and our life force. How we breathe, determines how we live. Becoming aware of breath, we breathe more slowly and deeply. We enter into the present moment, turn within, and realise the connection between breath and our subtle energy.

Breath slowing down

There is a tradition that every mammal has an allocated number of breaths. In this tradition the slower we breathe, the longer we live! The more aware we are of our breath, the slower we breathe and the more we relax and re-energise.

Full in-breath

To arrive at a full in-breath, we first concentrate on breathing into the solar plexus. We feel the expansion and contraction of the abdomen, caused by the lowering and rising of the diaphragm. This concentration ensures we fill the lower lungs with air, using their full capacity. Second, we become aware of the expansion of the ribcage, sideways around the heart. Third, we become aware of the subtle rise and fall of the shoulders. These three movements constitute the 'Full Yogic Breath'. If in doubt, just concentrate on the abdomen. For stressed people, deep abdominal breathing is the most important practice, as it corrects the imbalance caused by shallow breathing into the chest and shoulders only.

Full out-breath

To arrive at a full out-breath, practise sometimes breathing out so much that your abdomen pushes right in. This is not a regular habit - just an exercise to get the feeling of full exhalation. Unless we release our stale air we can never completely breathe in.

Warming up and loosening the lungs

To clear and warm the nasal passages, the yogic practise of Kapalabhati can be practised. The breath is pushed out of the nose in short puffs, pushing the stomach muscles in, with each breath. The abdomen spontaneously relaxes after each exhalation, causing the air to flow back in. Concentration is only on the out-breaths. After 10 such puffs, breathe in and out several times, deeply and slowly, and relax. You can practise several rounds. If you feel dizzy, you are over forcing the out-breath, and not replenishing your oxygen enough.

Purifying and balancing our energy through breath

To balance and purify the subtle energy system, 'Anuloma Viloma' can be practised. Place the right-hand thumb on the right nostril, index and ring fingers between the eyes, and fourth finger on the left nostril. Breathe in, through the left nostril, and out through the right nostril, and then in through the right and out through the left, until you feel completely comfortable both sides. Then breathe naturally through both nostrils, feeling your left and right body, brain and nervous systems, in balance.

Stepping between the in-breath and the out-breath

Mystically speaking, the in-breath and the out-breath, correlate to the contraction and expansion of the universe, the inflow and outflow of the breath of God, and creation and destruction. After the in-breath, it is possible to practise breath suspension for a few seconds, entering into the feeling of eternity, beyond time and space, movement and conditioning. If the breath is held, after breathing in, you will notice your vital energy builds up. No energy is wasted in movement, but you are still in being. It is very important not to strain during breath retention. The feeling is like dropping off and letting go. Ideally this condition happens naturally sometimes, when in profound meditative ecstasy. Used with Anuloma Viloma, breath suspension can be practised after the in-breath, on each side. Yogis often use the ratio of breathing in, for 2 counts, holding the breath for 8 counts, and breathing out for 4 counts, when practising Anuloma Viloma. Practise first from side to side, then with both nostrils breathing freely together.

Spiritual significance of breath

Our breath is closer to us than our dearest beloved. It is our connection to the Cosmos. It flows as oxygen in our veins. With each out-breath, we let go, relax, release and expand. With each in-breath, we replenish, build up, gather ourselves together, revitalize, contract. Mystically speaking, we die with each out-breath and are reborn with each in-breath. Every new breath is a new day, era, life and universe. Breath is a carrier of vital energy, Prana, and Chi. It is a gift received, as oxygen, from the Cosmos and symbolises the grace of the Divine Spirit that gifts us life itself. Learning to breathe well, we learn to live well. Harnessing this connection between body and soul, we can harness the secrets of life itself.

SVATMARAMA

'Life is said to exist only so long as there is breath in the body; its departure is death. So one should restrain the breath.'

PATANJALI

'Pranayama is the regulation of the incoming and outgoing flow of breath with retention. It is to be practised only after perfection in Asana is attained.'

'Pranayama has three movements. Prolonged and fine inhalation, exhalation and retention; all regulated with precision according to duration and place.'

'The fourth type of Pranayama transcends the external and internal pranayamas, and appears effortless and non deliberate.'

RUMI

'To place You in my heart may turn You into a thought. I will not do that! To hold you with my eyes may turn you into a thorn. I will not do that! I will set you on my breath so you will become my life!'

BUDDHA

'It is like this, the practitioner goes into the forest or to the foot of a tree, or to any deserted place, and sits stably in the cross-legged position, holding ones' body quite straight. Breathing in, one knows that one is breathing in; and breathing out, one knows that one is breathing out.'

GENESIS

'Then the Lord God formed man of dust from the ground, and breathed into his nostrils the breath of life; and man became a living being.'

JESUS

'After saying this he (Jesus) breathed on them and said: "Receive the Holy Spirit.'

BAHA'U'LLAH

'O people who are awakened by the breath of God. O people who are inhaling the scent of life from the Spirit of God...'

MEDITATION 10
LETTING GO – BREATHING OUT- SIGHING

Become aware of your breathing. Observe your breathing slowing down. Concentrate on your out-breath. Every time you breathe out, feel that you are letting go.

Let out a great sigh, as you breathe out. Feel the sigh emerge from your heart. Let go of all the concerns of your heart. Consciously let go of all your troubles.

Every time you breathe out, let go of the past. Let go of past traumas. Let go of past conflicts and tensions. Every time you breathe out, let go of the future. Of all your expectations about what could, should or would happen. Of all your worries about what you don't want to happen. Of all your fears about what you might be asked to do.

Every time you breathe out, let go of your stresses and strains. Imagine blockages in your body, mind and heart melting, like ice into water, washing away into the ground.

Become aware of the connection between your spine or feet and the ground. Each time you breathe out, feel the earth receiving and recycling all your difficulties, as it recycles waste material in nature.

Allow your abdomen to go right in, as you breathe out, pushing out the last piece of stagnant air. Feel, as you breathe out, that you are becoming emptier, lighter and increasingly free.

Form your left hand into a fist, enclosing the thumb in your fingers and place it on your abdomen. Form your right hand into a fist, but with your first finger free, pointing forward. Block your right nostril with your right finger, and breathe out through your left nostril. Feel your left fist move in with your abdomen, as you breathe out. Visualize black smoke emerging from your left nostril, expelling all dark thoughts and feelings. As you breathe in, visualize white light descending from above, filling your whole body. Repeat a number of times with each nostril, breathing out stale air and heavy psychic energy, from both sides of your body and psyche.

Now, removing your hands, fill your whole body with a wonderful new breath of air, oxygen, light and vitality, as you breathe in and just be.

MEDITATION 11
HEIGHT, DEPTH AND BREADTH

Breathing in, become aware of the point on the tip of your nose where the air enters your nostrils. Concentrate on the height dimension of your breath. As the air enters through your head, attune to the sensation of the air arriving from above. Become aware of the flow of moving air molecules, rippling up into, and down from, the stratosphere. Connect to the transcendental dimension of your being. Imagine your whole head is breathing in. Imagine you are breathing in, and out, through your crown chakra, at the top of your head. In the full yogic breath, we become aware of our shoulders rising and falling with our breathing. Connect this movement with the vertical dimension of your being.

Now become aware of the breadth of your breathing. Feel the air, as it travels to the back of the throat and down into the lungs, exchanging oxygen with carbon dioxide, in the blood that flows through the heart. Become aware of your chest expanding sideways, like the wings of a bird, as you expand and contract your lungs. Feel your heart, surrounded by the life giving energy of the air, through your lungs. Feel that your whole body is breathing. Become aware of the cells in your body exchanging oxygen and carbon dioxide with the environment. Realise that the process doesn't stop at the edge of your skin. The process of breathing has an effect which travels out into your environment and ultimately the cosmos. Breathing out, you embrace the universe and breathing in, the universe embraces you. You are the centre of a wonderful exchange of energy. Imagine a dot on a radar screen, sending out waves in all directions. That dot is your heart. As you breathe out, your heart is expanding, reaching out in wider circles. The whole cosmos is having a conversation with you, through your heart.

Now become aware of the depth of your breathing. Breathe deeply into your solar plexus. Draw the breath deep down into your being, into your abdomen. Some traditions call this 'Deep Belly Breathing'. Feel you are journeying in and down through your breathing. Allow your consciousness to be calmed by the expansion and contraction of your abdomen, as you breathe deeply. Feel your whole nervous system slowing down. Feel that you are dropping off to a sublime place, deep within. Relax. Images may come to mind emerging from within. Just be aware. Just be.

MEDITATION 12
ANULOMA VILOMA WITH LIGHT

We can combine our breathing practices with meditation on light and even sound. Really there are no stages in meditation. Each stage contains, within it, all the stages, as every moment contains, within it, eternity. As we practise one concentration, we may experience new dimensions open up within us, revealing new concentrations.

Relax deeply with a straight spine and deep abdominal breathing. Lift your right hand. Place your right thumb on your right nostril. Place your 2nd and 3rd finger on your forehead. Place your 4th finger on your left nostril. Breathe in through the left nostril, blocking the right nostril, and then out through the right nostril, blocking the left nostril. Then, back in through the right nostril, blocking the left nostril, and out the left nostril, blocking the right. In this way, alternate your in-breath continuously, from left to right, and then right to left, until you are breathing freely, on both sides. Having balanced the left and right sides of your breath and nervous system, introduce breath retention, after the in-breath. Practise every day, for a short period of time, until you are comfortable breathing in for 2 counts, holding for 8 counts, and breathing out for 4 counts. Once you are comfortable on each side with the breath counts, finish the counting practice without hands, breathing both sides at once. Only do the breath retention for a limited number of breaths. Afterwards breathe naturally, lightly and easily, feeling buoyant and balanced.

Now introduce light visualization to your practice. Breathing in the left side, imagine light spiralling up your spine, from left to right. Breathing in the right side, imagine light spiralling up your spine, from right to left. Breathing in both sides, imagine light spiralling up your spine, both ways. Holding your breath, feel light travelling up through your skull into the transcendent dimension, above. Breathing out, feel the descent of light, the breath of God, the Holy Spirit, coming down. If you have a mantra, you can repeat the mantra as you breathe up, and down, your spine. You can repeat the mantra in the suspension of breath. You can feel the Word of the One Being descending, as you breathe out.

Don't forget to end your meditation simply by sitting, being, listening and feeling the response of the universe, and yourself, to the practice.

MEDITATION 13
RISING THROUGH THE ELEMENTS

Breathing in through the mouth, cools us down, compared to breathing in through the nose, where we have hairs to break down, and warm up, the air. A Sufi practice combines varying mouth and nasal breathing, with travelling through the spectrum of the elements, refining and expanding our consciousness as we go.

Breathe in and out through the nose and concentrate on the earth element. Concentrate on the connection between the base of your spine and the earth. Remember that your body arose from the earth and will return to the earth. Feel you are breathing in the earth's vitality, through your spine, as a tree draws up nutrients through its roots. Feel as you breathe out, that all your negative and imbalanced energy is being recycled and reprocessed by Mother Earth. Feel your firm foundation on Mother Earth.

Breathe in through the nose and out through the mouth, concentrating on the water element. As you breathe in, visualize and hear a fountain of water, raising life giving energy up your spine. As you breathe out, imagine water flowing down on you from above, washing away tensions and inner blockages. Visualize yourself flowing freely and flexibly in life, meeting all the challenges and changes you come across.

Breathe in through the mouth and out through the nose, concentrating on the element of fire. Breathing in, visualize a flame rising up your spine. Imagine the flame travelling through the light spectrum through red, orange, yellow, green, blue, and purple. Feel heavy energy in you being burnt up and sparked into life. Breathing out, imagine brilliant white light descending on you from above. Breathing out, feel yourself radiating light in all directions. Imagine yourself meeting life's challenges with passion, and vitality.

Breathe in and out through the mouth very gently, with the lips just slightly apart. Feel the coolness and lightness of your breathing. Concentrate on the element of air. Visualize a feather slow falling, an eagle circling the mountain heights, a yogi high on a mountain filled with expansive consciousness. Rise above the conditions of your life.

Returning to nasal breathing, attune to the element of ether which holds all the other elements. Attune to the space within and around everything. Letting go completely, just be.

STAGE FOUR

DOORWAYS TO THE SOUL BREATH AWAKENING ENERGY CENTRES

This beautiful cactus evokes the 1000 petalled lotus chakra, which, according to Yoga, is located at the top of the head.

YOGIC WORD
CHAKRA SADHANA

Just as Lucy walked through the back of a cupboard into a magical world, in "The Lion, the Witch and the Wardrobe", we can discover a reality of unlimited dimensions through the Heart, and learn to live on many levels at once.

FOLLOWING OUR BREATH THROUGH THE DOORWAY OF THE HEART

As we become aware of our breathing, we can start meditating on the direction of our breath, focusing on energy centres in the body.

We can imagine we are breathing up, and down, the spine. We can imagine we are breathing in, and out, of our heart centre. We can imagine breath is descending from the head, down into the solar plexus, and up and out of the heart centre.

According to Yoga, we have focal points in our body which are doorways into different dimensions of being. As we can become aware of our breath, we can imagine it flowing into, around and between, different energy centres in our body - like the 7 increasingly well known 'chakra' centres of the spine, or the three primary centres in the head, heart and solar plexus.

In the Yogic tradition, it is understood that breath and oxygen carry light and vitality called 'Prana', in India, or 'Chi', in the Chinese tradition. If we want to heal, revitalize or awaken a part of ourselves, we concentrate on that area when breathing. If we concentrate on our heart, as we breathe in, our experience of our feeling centre grows. Our consciousness becomes more expansive, sensitive and responsive. If we concentrate on our head, as we breathe in, our experience of our thinking clarifies and we may awaken spiritual vision and wisdom. If we concentrate on our solar plexus, as we breathe in, our experience of deeper levels of our being develops, and our nervous system and intuitive gut instinct is ignited, strengthened and revitalized. Using body centres to function in life is a common practice. Think of these three phrases commonly used: "In your heart of hearts, what do you feel about it?" "What is your gut instinct? Should we go for it?" "What do you think you're doing? Use your head!"

Focusing first on the 7 chakras, awakening the flow of energy, we can zone into the 3 primary centres, finally coming to rest in the one centre of centres - the Heart. Jesus always referred to the heart as the primary centre in the temple of the Holy Spirit called the body. Jesus, Mary, Mohammed, Fatima, Buddha, Rama, Krishna, Siva and Sita all agree that the heart is the centre of centres in the body, and if in doubt, the Way of the Heart is always the surest, safest and sweetest road.

BUDDHA
'With single mindedness the Master quells his thoughts. He ends their wandering. Seated in the cave of the heart, he finds freedom.'
'The way is not in the sky. The way is in the heart.'

JESUS
'Blessed are the pure in heart, for they shall see God.'
'A good man draws what is good from the store of goodness in his heart.'

ST SYMEON THE NEW THEOLOGIAN
'For as soon as the intellect attains the place of the heart, at once it sees things of which it previously knew nothing. It sees the open space within the heart and it beholds itself entirely luminous and full of discrimination.'

KRISHNA
'God dwells in the heart of all beings, Arjuna: thy God dwells in thy heart.'
'Seekers of union, ever striving, see him dwelling in their own hearts.'

RUMI
'Deafened by the voice of desire, you are unaware the Beloved lives in the core of your heart. Stop the noise, and you will hear his voice in the silence.'

ST NICEPHORUS OF MOUNT ATHOS
'You are aware that our breathing by which we live is an inhaling and exhaling of air. The organs that serve for this purpose are the lungs which surround the heart. They pass air through themselves and flood the heart with it. Thus breathing is the natural way to the heart.'

UPANISHADS
'How can we roll up the sky like a piece of deerskin? How can we end our misery without realising that the Lord of Love is enshrined in our heart of hearts?'

MEDITATION 14
BREATHING LIGHT IN THREE DIRECTIONS

IN AND OUT – REACHING OUT

Breathe in and out of your heart centre. Feel your heart at the centre of the Cosmos, like the dot at the centre of a radar screen. As you breathe out, expand your breath out in all directions. As you breathe in, feel the breath of the Cosmos breathing into your heart centre. Visualize your breath as white light. Feel your heart as the centre of an expanding and contracting ball of light. Feel that you are a star radiating and drawing in light from all around. Breathing in, recall everyone who loves you. Breathing out, recall all those whom you love. Sit in the centre of an everlasting exchange of love.

UP AND DOWN – REACHING UP

Imagine, as you breathe in, that you are breathing up your spine. Imagine, as you breathe out, that the breath is returning down your spine. As you breathe in, imagine you are gathering and lifting up, all the heavy energy at the base of your spine. As you breathe out, imagine fresh energy descending. Feel the connection between the base of your spine and the magnetic energy of the earth. As you breathe in, feel you are drawing this energy up your spine and out the top of your head into the Cosmos. As you breathe out, feel as if the Cosmos is breathing down on your head. Visualize your breath as brilliant, white light. Feel yourself drawing the light up your spine and into the Cosmos, as if sending up a light or a prayer. As you breathe out, feel starlight descending, as a Cosmic answer to your prayer. As you breathe in, draw in and up, your highest aspiration and send it flying heavenwards. As you breathe out, feel the universe opening doors, in answer to your deepest wishes.

DOWN UP AND OUT – GRACE TRANSFORMING

As you breathe in, feel the breath of the universe descending as grace on the top of your skull, like a waterfall of white light, flowing down into your abdomen. As you breathe out, feel the breath rising to your heart and expanding out in all directions. See yourself at the centre of a circle of light, travelling down and within and then up and without. Imagine you are collecting the light of the stars and the Cosmos, as you breathe in, and then returning the light back out to the Cosmos through your heart. Breathing in and down, ask yourself 'What does the universe ask of me? Breathing up and out, ask yourself 'and what am I doing about it?'

MEDITATION 15
RISING THROUGH THE LIGHT SPECTRUM

One of the easiest ways to bring a natural, buoyant energy into the body, is to meditate on colour. The colours of the rainbow are formed by the diffraction of white light. By evoking each colour of the rainbow, we rediscover the balance of the one light, which contains all colours. By travelling up the colour spectrum we lift and expand our consciousness from heavier, warmer vibrations to cooler, more subtle, vibrations. By bathing in all the colours of the light spectrum, and the energetic vibrations those colours contain, we re-adjust any energy imbalances in our system. Meditation on colour is a form of colour therapy. It is a universal method that uses our shared experience of colour to re-align our consciousness.

As you meditate on colour, keep four images in your consciousness. A flame of light rising up your spine, a journey from the centre of the earth to the edge of the Cosmos, the journey through the stages of life and the pyramid of human needs. The interconnectedness of different dimensions in life is a key experience in meditation.

Imagine the colour red. Become aware of the base of your spine. Feel a red flame rising up your spine. Imagine you are in the hot core of the earth. Imagine your body and the universe is filled with the colour red. Breathe red in, and out. Red evokes passion for life, the colour of blood and our basic vitality and drive. Observe any reactions in your consciousness to the colour red. Recall your basic needs as a human being - food, shelter and survival, and the baby stage of life when survival is the priority. Focus on the element earth.

Imagine the flame travelling up your spine to the area of the reproductive organs, turning to orange. Visualize your body and the universe filled with orange, and breathe the colour in, and out. Imagine travelling out from the centre of the earth. Orange relates to our relationships in life. Recall the stage of dependence in life, when we need our parents and siblings – our 'tribe'. Become aware of our need to belong, move, give and take in life, fulfil desires, earn money and make decisions rather than just survive. Connect to the element of sustenance and flow - water.

Now feel the flame travel further up and turn yellow. Connect to the solar plexus chakra. Bathe in yellow, breathing the colour in, and out. Feel that you are about to break through the earths' crust, as you travel out from the centre of the earth. The solar plexus is the radiant, powerful, sun centre of our nervous system. Recall the stage in life when we become independent of our family and discover our own rhythm and voice. Focus on the fire element.

Now break through onto the surface of the planet. Connect to your heart chakra. Feel the flame turn green. Breathe green in, and out. Feel the quality of love and our need to help those around us. Recall the stage of interdependence in life, when we decide to get together with others, not out of weakness and dependence, but so as to pool our strengths. Perhaps the time in life when we fall in love and raise our own family, or when we discover our passion and vocation of service in life. The green vegetation on the surface of the earth, is the meeting place between the forces of earth rising, and the forces of heaven descending.

Now travel further up the spine to the throat centre, the flame turning blue. Imagine you are entering the higher regions of the clear blue sky. Feel the transformation of your energy to a more subtle, expansive and cooler feeling. Blue connects us to clarity, clear communication, and higher creativity. Recall times in life when we create something that has a life of its own, like a book, a song, a garden, or even a child. Become aware of our need to leave a legacy in life, to tell a story, and to reach out to humanity on a larger scale than our immediate surroundings, friends and family.

Now travel further up, beyond the earth, into the celestial regions. Visualize the celestial and royal colour purple. Focus on the pineal gland area, in the back of the head. Recall the purple pictures of star systems and the cosmos, and imagine you are seeing things from a vaster perspective. Purple relates to spiritual wisdom. Recall the moments in life when we have realisations, illuminations and insights, as part of our one-on-one relationship with the universe, which make our life ultimately meaningful.

Become aware of the place where the top of your skull meets the sky. Visualize brilliant white light, which also seems to shimmer with, and contain all, the colours of the rainbow, surrounding and penetrating your whole body. Feel as if the edges of your body have dissolved, and there is only one brilliant white light. Attune to the stage of surrender, peace and fulfilment in life.

Flowers are natures' Yantras (Sacred shapes). They heal us both through their harmonious structural beauty, and their beautiful spectrums of colour. Gazing on a flower will unfurl the beauty within your heart centre, soothing your body, mind and soul with harmony and light.

47

MEDITATION 16
VIBRATING ENERGY CENTRES WITH SOUND

Sit in a meditation posture, and become aware of your deep breathing. Start to chant the mantra 'Aum' out loud (see next section for more about mantras). The letter 'A' represents the beginning of sound, as you open your mouth. The letter 'M' represents the end of sound, as you close your mouth. The letter 'U' represents the continuing expression of sound. Altogether the mantra 'AUM' represents the full spectrum of sound, and the sound of sound - the Word, that was in the beginning. You can also use 'Amen' (Christian) or 'Amin' (Islam) from the Western traditions, if you prefer.

Chant the sound and listen to the sound, at the same time. Feel the sound vibrating in your whole body. Imagine that the atoms in your body are being shaken up and energised by the sound of the mantra. Imagine your atoms dancing. Feel the sound rising from deep in your solar plexus, filling your whole body and the whole room with sound. Connect your personal 'Aum' with the 'Cosmic Aum' in the room. Feel as if you are giving your whole body, spirit and mind a sound scan, with the energy of the mantra 'Aum'. Visualize the energy radiating out in circles from your abdomen and returning back to you, as echoes from all directions. You are at the centre of a vibrant, harmonious and uplifting sound wave.

Bring your awareness to your first chakra, at the base of the spine. Concentrate on this centre as you chant and vibrate the sound 'Aum'. Repeat this process in each of the seven chakras, ending at the crown chakra. You can add two further positions. Start your first 'Aum', vibrating the whole planet Mother Earth, below your first Chakra. Finish your ninth AUM, above your head, representing the Transcendent dimension, above and beyond, called the 'Father' in many traditions.

Now bring the AUM mantra back down the chakras. Starting at the crown of the head and coming down all the seven chakras to the ground. Feel the spirit coming down, balancing the chakra energy centres.

Now sit silently, resting in your being, experiencing the effects of your practise. Slowly stretch and rotate your neck, shoulders, hands and feet feeling your energy being grounded and naturalised in movement.

STAGE FIVE

VISION OF LIGHT
VISUAL CONCENTRATION

Inside St.Peters' Basilica in Rome

YOGIC WORD – YANTRA DHARANA

Many people who have had an after-death experience, talk about walking down a dark tunnel, towards a light. Imagine you are in that dark tunnel. Imagine you can see the light, shining in the distance. Visualize yourself walking towards that light, which grows in size, as you approach. Arriving at the light, imagine your surprise when, merging with the light, you realize you have reconnected to something deeply familiar – the incredible light of your own being.

TRAVELLING IN A BODY OF LIGHT

Up until this point, we have used our personal body as a sacred and natural form, a temple, to meditate on, a doorway into greater dimensions of being, following the edict that 'the Kingdom of Heaven is within'. Now we use our mind to go beyond our personal body identification. We expand and extend our consciousness, concentrating on universal and archetypal forms found in nature and in the soul of humanity. In the balance of the elements, the perfection of a flower, the lives of Masters, Saints and Prophets, we find examples of where we have come from, and who we could be. We reach beyond ourselves, reaching out to the stars, our Father in Heaven, and back to the first Adam, our roots in nature and Mother Earth. Meditating on a candle flame, on light itself, on a Mandala or Yantra, the natural form of a tree or mountain, or the face of an enlightened being, we extend and expand our boundaries.

As we meditate deeply, we enter the inner void, the far reaches of outer space - what a Christian mystic called the 'Cloud of Unknowing'. It is a mind-blowing journey, and to remain stable and safe we need to chart our path through inner space using light forms, just as sea travellers use stars in the sky to plot their journey.

Our mind is conditioned to concentrate on forms, jumping from one to another, fascinated by the variety of life. Yoga calls this tendency the 'Monkey Mind', and instead of working against the minds natural attraction to forms, advocates using this mental ability to focus. By focusing the mind continuously on one point, one form, we learn to steady the mind, and eventually still the mind completely, so that we can enter our heart space. There is a second aspect to this. Whatever we focus on, begins to manifest, at first inwardly and eventually outwardly. So Yoga advocates that we choose uplifting and harmonious light forms to meditate on.

We may meditate on pure, white light. We may concentrate on particular symbols, like a star with a crescent moon. We may meditate on a geometric form, a Yantra, a Mandala. We may concentrate on a sacred being, and particularly his or her face, or profile. In these ways, we identify not just with our personal body, but with an archetypal body. It's like getting out of our car and sitting down in a supersonic jet, to travel with our fellow human beings to a common destination.

BUDDHA

'Beware of the anger of the mind. Master your thoughts. Let them serve the truth.'

JESUS

'The eye is the lamp of the body. So if your eye is sound, your whole body will be full of light. But if your eye is not sound, your whole body will be full of darkness.'

'While you have the light, believe in the light, that you may become sons of light.'

KRISHNA

'He is the light of all lights which shines beyond all darkness. It is vision, the end of vision, to be reached by vision, dwelling in the heart of all.'

'When the mind of the Yogi is in harmony and finds rest in the Spirit within, all restless desires gone, then he is a Yukta, One in God. Then his soul is a lamp whose light is steady, for it burns in a shelter where no winds come.'

PATANJALI

'Fixing the consciousness on one point or region is concentration.'

'And whenever the mind unsteady and restless strays away from the Spirit, let him ever and for ever lead it again to the Spirit.'

UPANISHADS

'The Self in man and in the Sun are one. Those who understand this see through the world and go beyond the various sheaths of being to realize the unity of life.'

HAFIZ

'I wish I could show you, when you are lonely or in darkness, the astonishing light of your own being!'

MEDITATION 17
CANDLE FLAME CONCENTRATION

The first step in light meditation is to light a candle. A candle light is the outward manifestation of the inner light. It connects us to the archetypal tradition of fire ceremonies, going back to the days when we lived out, in nature, and used fire to create a warm, safe place of comfort and friendship. The moment humankind harnessed fire, we lit the light of our soul's aspiration for greater brilliance. Nearly every major world spiritual tradition uses candle light to meditate. For the human being, where there is the possibility of fire, there is the possibility of life. Food can be cooked, animals can be scared away and pathways can be illuminated in the darkness. Whatever we look at, creates a resonance in our inner being. As we stare at a candle flame, we experience an affirmation of the light within us. Burning in the darkness, a candle is a symbol of the human condition. We are lights of consciousness, burning in the huge darkness of the cosmos. If we feel enveloped in darkness, simply to light and stare at a candle, is a most concrete and effective way to turn our consciousness around. We can train our consciousness in this way. A candle flame is one of the easiest objects to concentrate on, because it dances continuously, and is instantly absorbing.

Sitting still, gently focus your attention on the candle flame. Allow your eyes simply to rest on your object of concentration. Do not examine the flame with your mind. Allow the flame to talk to you and touch you. Feel the flame. Simply receive the impression of the flame onto your retina. Imagine you have never seen anything before. Do not think about the flame. Allow your consciousness simply to rest on the flame - steadily, continuously and gently. If your mind or eyes wander, don't worry. Bring them back continuously to the flame. It is more important not to worry than to focus rigidly. If you can sit like this for 10 minutes you will experience a change in your consciousness. Do not censor anything you experience. Learn from everything. The candle light will reveal things to you. Ideas will pop into your head. Do not dismiss them. Use them later when you return to the field of activity. But do not follow the ideas. Keep returning to the candle flame. The flame is your guide, your protection, your circle of warmth. Keep training your consciousness consistently, calmly, happily to focus on this point of illumination.

MEDITATION 18
EXPANDING THE ONE LIGHT

This meditation connects our expanded experience of ourselves with spreading the one light, to help all. Begin this meditation by centring in, on your body, breath and heart. Surround yourself with a blanket of glowing, warm, golden-tinged white light. Allow this light to immunise you from the difficult circumstances of your life, which, for this moment, are in the past. Imagine your heart is a cave, holding a sacred space within you. In the darkness of that cave, light your inner candle flame. Whatever happens in your life, this light can warm your heart and shine out of your eyes.

Now visualize your candle radiating light. Feel the light expanding beyond the safety of the cave in your heart centre. See the light filling your body. Feel your body now beginning to radiate light so that the edges of your form melt and blur, in the lights radiance. Feel the light expanding to an aura of light surrounding your body. Realise that your body is indeed surrounded by an electro-magnetic field, and that you are now attuning to that reality. Let the light expand further. Consciously think of someone who needs more light and more love - who is suffering and experiencing darkness in their life. Now surround that person with this golden light. Visualize the circumstances of this person's life changing for the better. See that person smiling, bathed in this healing energy. Repeat this process with a place in the world that is suffering, and Mother Earth herself, in desperate need of our light and love.

Now feel the light expanding out beyond the planet into the galaxy. Become aware of the radiance of the sun and the glittering panoply of stars, radiating light. Become aware that we are all star dust, born out of the birth of stars. Realise that the light in your heart, originated in the light of the stars, and the light of the stars is only visible through the light in your heart. Realise that the light of intelligence in you, is the intelligence behind the light of the stars. Experience a wonderful exchange of energising light with the stars, and feel your sense of yourself expanded to a cosmic degree.

Now allow the light to return to its source in your heart centre. Feel the light withdrawing from the stars and planets to the earth. From the earth, to your country and town and people you know. Finally to your body and heart centre, completing this cycle of expansion and contraction in light and love.

MEDITATION 19
FOCUSING ON A SYMBOL

Choose a symbol that draws you and attracts you at this moment. Perhaps it is a photo of a flower or a scene in nature. Perhaps it is a photo of a mosc, temple or church or the face of Jesus, Buddha, Siva, Mary or an innocent child. Perhaps it is a Mandala or Yantra, like the Sri Chakra (see opposite), or a beautiful tree you may know. Choose your symbol now. With your eyes open rest your awareness on that symbol. Notice every detail you possibly can, making sure you are awake, alive, sharp and alert. Keep focusing.

Now shift your point of view. Instead of looking from the point of view of knowledge of the object, pretend you are a new baby, who knows nothing. Become passive in your observation. Let your awareness simply rest on the object taking in the whole picture at once. Allow it to speak to you, rather than thinking that you are looking at it. As you become absorbed in the image, forget yourself, lost in the object of your contemplation. As your awareness rests on its object, feel more and more, and think less and less. Experience the 'presence' of the image - the feeling behind the image. See if you can look with your heart and feel the qualities that the image is radiating - the inner life and spirit of the object. Perhaps you can see the aura of the image, which comes with its feeling.

Now close your eyes holding the image and its feeling. If you feel yourself forgetting the image and the experience waning, open your eyes again, to re-impress the image on your retina, mind and soul. Then close your eyes again. Holding the feeling of the image, the experience of presence you are now experiencing, let go of the visual image. Rest now, solely, in the presence. You have travelled beyond the form of creation to the feeling of creation. From the particular image, to its presence, and then to presence itself. You are on a journey to the source of feeling and presence - the One Creator. Ride the wave of this awareness, as far as it takes you. You can at any time retrace your steps, if you feel yourself losing your concentration and awareness.

Now finally open your eyes and look again at the object. See if you can see the details of the image, feel the presence of the image, and feel the presence of the One, all at the same time. If you can do this, you are experiencing enlightened awareness with eyes open, in the world. This is the final goal of meditation.

This image is called the 'Sri Chakra Yantra.' It is one of the most complete and revered sacred, geometric images. Amongst other things, it is a diagram of the complete human being, and contains within its structure all the stages of life. Every tradition has its Yantras. In Christianity the Cross is the symbol of victory over death. For many people the Heart is a universal symbol of love. The Sufi Order, for example, uses the symbol of a Heart with two wings.

MEDITATION 20
SYMBOLS AS DOORWAYS INTO THE SACRED

You can use concentration on symbols to ignite, foster and deepen spiritual awareness. The experience doesn't stop there. Focusing on symbols leads to experiences of related sounds and feelings. The symbols we focus on change our experience of life. Surrounding ourselves with positive uplifting images will transform our state of mind. Every spiritual place of worship uses this principle.

Become aware now of your head centre as you breathe in and out. Visualize a golden egg - a symbol of the birth of Cosmic Consciousness - at the back of your head, where the pineal gland is located in the human brain. Imagine that the egg is infinitely small and infinitely radiant, manifesting golden effulgent light in all directions. Breathe that light in, and out, of your head. Visualize Siva, and silently repeat the word 'Truth', three times. Siva is the image evoked by Yogis sitting cross-legged in the snowy Himalayas, representing self-mastery and uncompromising concentration on the Truth of Being, beyond all duality. You can use a sacred mantra that evokes this quality. For example 'Om Namah Sivaya' or 'Ya Haqq' (truth in Arabic) or 'Abba'–Father (Hebrew). Breathing in, and out, attune to the feeling of clarity.

Now breathe in, and out, of your abdomen. Visualize a perfect full moon, deep in your core centre. Visualize the quality of moonlight - peaceful, reflective light. Visualize a full moon perfectly reflected in a calm lake. As you breathe in, and out, focus on the word 'Peace', or repeat sacred words for peace, such as Shantih (Sanskrit) or Salaam (Arabic) or Shalom (Hebrew). Feel the quality of an ever deepening peace. Visualize a sacred being evoking peace, such as Buddha.

Now breathe in, and out, of your heart centre. Visualize the radiant sun in your heart centre. Feel the sunlight radiating out in all directions, as you breathe in, and out. Silently repeat the word 'Love', or use a sacred word that evokes this quality, like 'Prema' (love in Sanskrit), 'Maranatha' (Come Lord Jesus, come in Aramaic) or 'Ya Waduud' (the give and take of love in Arabic). You can visualize a sacred being like Christ, Quan Yin, or Krishna. Feel love embracing you, and feel yourself embracing all with love, as you breathe in, and out. Rest now in a state of perfect balance, and allow your own spontaneous realisation to unfold.

STAGE SIX

RIDING THE WAVE OF SOUND
SOUND CONCENTRATION

YOGIC WORD – MANTRA DHARANA

Placing your hands above your head, sing the Sufi mantra 'Amin', and run your hands down your body, feeling the descent of divine blessings. Placing your hands in prayer position, chant the Christian mantra 'Amen', feeling devotion, in your heart. Placing your hands on your lap, chant the Hindu mantra 'Aum', feeling yourself melting, in Peace.

Sound soothes the body/mind complex into submission, keeping the mind focussed and the heart singing, while the soul gently reveals itself, like the rising sun. You don't need a mantra from a tradition you don't understand. Every tradition uses mantras, and every human has an inner dialogue.

TRAVELLING BEYOND THE SEEN

When we close our eyes, we can still hear. In mystical traditions, sound takes us further along the mystical path than light. In the Desert Fathers tradition of the Jesus Prayer, the name of Jesus is repeated without the visualization of any form. It is believed that negative forces can appear misleadingly in a sacred form, but crumble without resistance when confronted with the actual name of Jesus. If we look at the sun with our eyes, we are blinded and see nothing. But with sound waves, scientists can study the echoes, and understand the structure, of the sun. This is the principle of mantra. We leave light particles behind and travel on sound waves, to go further. Sound breaks down rigid forms and gets us into the state of flow. That is why music gets us all dancing and brings different cultures together, in a universal, unifying language of the heart.

Every spiritual tradition uses sound. In the Sufi tradition this is called Wazifa, in the Yogic tradition 'Mantra', and in the Christian - Judaic tradition, the 'Name' or the 'Word'. The most powerful mantras are in a spiritual language such as Sanskrit, Hebrew, or Arabic. These languages were created from a mystical perspective and the sound syllables vibrate with the mantras meanings. Using a spiritual language has the added advantage of bypassing our usual conscious way of thinking, and gives us quicker access to the Collective Unconscious (read Carl Jung for more) and the Superconscious mind (the Yogic word for the Divine Mind). In addition, words used for centuries to evoke a spiritual principle, have the power of the practise of millions of devoted souls behind them, carving a pathway through the archetypal mind of humanity. In this sense, Latin has also become a very powerful spiritual language, evoking Christ's presence for 2000 years.

It is very powerful to combine mantra with breath. Our mantra then becomes closer to us than our very breath. We can also repeat the mantra when holding the breath. The purpose of mantra is to take us beyond form. When we travel beyond form, we can lose our bearings. Sacred sound gives us something reliable to hold onto. In the end, sacred sound is not about location or even breath. We simply concentrate on the mantra and nothing else. We travel back to the 'Word', that was in the beginning, before it became 'flesh'. The best advice at this stage, is to repeat the mantra, let go of everything else, and flow back to the source.

58

MANTRAS PURIFY AND TRANSFORM

By focusing on one thought, our Mantra, we become one pointed. We become purified of all the conflicting thoughts and troubles of our mind. At the same time, by concentrating on a positive and sacred sound, we transform our inner nature, planting positive seeds in our unconscious, helping us develop a more beautiful presence and personality. In contrast to the hypocrite, our inner life becomes more radiant than our outer form can express. In the garden of our heart, we plant the seeds of love. Here are some of the most well known mantras used in humankinds' inner journey.

Positive Affirmation – New Age Mantra
I love and approve of myself

Yogic Mantras Without Form
Aum(Hindu), Amen(Christian), or Amin(Islam)
Soham – 'I Am That I Am'

CHRISTIAN
Maranatha – Aramaic for 'Come Lord Jesus'.
Jesus Christ Son of God have mercy on me
Ave Maria
Kyrie Eleison Christe Eleison
BUDDHIST
Nam Myoho Renge Kyo
Om Mani Padme Hum
Gate Gate Paragate Parasamgate Bodhi Svaha
HINDU
Ram
Om Namah Sivaya
Sita Ram
Om Ma
ISLAMIC
Allah Hu
Bismillah ar Rahman ar Rahim
Ya Haqq – truth, being
Ya Wadud –give and take of love

Peace, Pax Christi, Shantih, Salaam, Shalom

JESUS

'When you pray say 'Father, hallowed be thy name'.
'If you continue in my word you are truly my disciples, and you will know the truth, and the truth will make you free.'
'Where two or three are gathered together in my name, there am I in the midst of them.'

KRISHNA

'I am OM, the sacred word of the Vedas, sound in silence, heroism in men.'
'If when a man leaves his earthly body he is in the silence of Yoga, and closing the doors of his soul, he keeps the mind in his heart, and places in the head the breath of life, and remembering me he utters OM, the eternal Word of Brahman, he goes to the path supreme.'

HAZRAT INAYAT KHAN

'There is nothing more important, as a means of raising one's consciousness, than the repetition of the right word; there is nothing that can be of greater use and importance in the path of spiritual attainment.'

RUMI

'Prayer clears the mist and brings back peace to the soul. Every morning, every evening let the heart sing 'La ilaha il Allah'-
There is no reality but God.'

BUDDHA

'Therefore know the perfection of wisdom is the great mantra, is the bright mantra, is the unsurpassed mantra, is the unequalled mantra that can remove all suffering, and is true not false. Therefore proclaim the Perfect Wisdom mantra. Proclaim the mantra that says: Gate, gate, paragate, parasamgate, bodhi, svaha!'

GURU NANAK

'The purest and sweetest essence is the Name which takes thee back to the eternal home.'

MEDITATION 21
NADA YOGA

Nada Yoga simply means 'union through sound'. Any use of mantra, sound, and sacred song is Nada Yoga. Taize chants, the Gayatri Mantra, the Salve Regina and Sufi Quawalis, are all forms for Nada Yoga, although they don't usually go by that name. One simple Nada Yoga practice, to balance and tune the body's vibrational system, involves chanting up and down the musical scale, and correlating this with the body's chakra system. This is a very effective and uplifting practice. Sung up and down the Western harmonic scale, seven seed sounds are used. This is excellent if you are feeling out of balance, heavy or even depressed. The seven notes are 'Sa', 'Re', 'Ga', 'Ma', 'Pa', 'Ta', and 'Ni'. The 'a' sound is pronounced 'ar', i.e. Sar, Gar, Mar, Par, and Tar. 'Re' is pronounced 'Ray' and 'Ni' is pronounced 'Nee'. 'Sa' is repeated again at the top of the scale.

Start focusing on the base of your spine, your root chakra. Chant Sa.
Focus on your reproductive chakra. Chant Re.
Focus on your solar plexus chakra. Chant Ga.
Focus on your heart chakra. Chant Ma
Focus on your throat chakra. Chant Pa.
Focus on your third eye chakra. Chant Ta.
Focus on your top of the skull chakra. Chant Ni.
Focus on the transcendent dimension. Chant again Sa.

Practise until you can feel each energy centre vibrating, in balanced harmony, as tuned by the seed sounds.
Practise ascending and descending your chakras.
Practise speeding up.
Practise ascending to 2nd chakra then down, to the 3rd, then down, to the 4th then down etc.
Practise lowering the first 'Sa' as low as you can.
Practise raising the scale as high as you can.
Practise out loud, then silently repeating the seed sounds.
Then, rest in your heart centre, feeling how your energy has been transformed, balanced and uplifted.

MEDITATION 22
SOUND HEALING

There are many forms of sound healing. Here are two beautiful examples.

YOGIC BIJA MANTRAS

These mantras, called 'Bija' - seed, mantras, can be self-prescribed for healing purposes. Each mantra creates a particular sound wave vibration, correlating to an energy centre in the body. Repeated, one after the other, up the spine, these mantras will uplift and rejuvenate our energy. Repeated in one particular area, the seed mantra will heal and strengthen that part of the body.

Physical Location	Chakra Name	Mantra
Base of Spine	Mooladhara	Lam
Reproductive area	Swadhisthana	Vam
Naval Centre	Manipura	Ram
Heart Centre	Anahata	Yam
Throat	Vishuddhi	Ham
Eyebrow Centre	Ajna	Om

SUFI WAZIFAS

Sufi Wazifas, coming from the mystical Islamic tradition, evoke and vibrate with, Divine Qualities of God. They are repeated, so as to foster and evoke these qualities in our lives. The idea is to develop a beautiful balance of sacred energies, in and around our body, mind, personality and soul, and to continually express them, and develop them, in our lives. Repetition of the whole sequence has a wonderful effect on our vital energy.

Chakra(see above)	Divine Quality	Wazifa
Mooladhara	Divine Patience	Ya Matin
Swadhisthana	Flowing blessings	Ya Wahaboo
Manipura	Self Mastery	Ya Wali
Anahata	Exalted	Ya Azziz
Visuddhi	Holy Spirit	Ya Quddus
Ajna	All knowing	Ya Alim
Sahasrara(top of skull)	Breath of God	Ya Hu

MEDITATION 23
THE HUMAN STORY IN SACRED SOUND

We are going on a journey through the evolution of human consciousness.

Let's start at the very beginning - in the nature traditions of our ancestors and indigenous peoples, who emphasized Mother Earth far more than we do today. Connect to your sense of the sacred feminine, the maternal, and the sacredness of creation itself. Repeat the Mantra '**Om Ma**', placing your awareness at the base of your spine, and then flow freely wherever the mantra takes you. Feel the love of the Divine Mother healing you, your family, friends, nation, and the planet.

Now travel to one of the oldest yogic traditions in the world and repeat the mantra '**Om Namah Sivaya**'. Place your awareness at the top of your head, attuning to your transcendent dimension - the 'Father' beyond all, and then let your awareness flow as it pleases. Connect to your inner 'Self', beyond all conditions, your inner yogic fire of self-mastery, and your eye of wisdom, which sees things how they are, without personal slant or vantage point.

Travel on now to the tradition of Buddhism, which emerged out of Hinduism. Centre your awareness in your abdomen, repeating the mantra '**Om Mani Padme Om**'. Connect to your inner depths. Enter into deeper and deeper levels of peace, well beyond the heat and frustrations of life's aims, objectives and desires.

Rise up now to your heart centre. Repeat the mantra '**Maranatha**', the Aramaic word for 'come Lord Jesus, come' and invite Jesus into your heart. Connect to this beautiful being of love, and radiate compassion out in all directions, from your heart centre, showering love on all, especially those least able to fend for themselves.

Journey on now, to the deserts and starlit night skies of the lands of Islam and Mohammed - the seal of the prophets. Breathe the mantra '**Allah**' up your spine, and breathe the mantra '**Hu**' down your spine. Offer up all your aspirations to the One Beloved, as you breathe 'Allah' in, and up. Feel his breath of mercy flowing down on you - a light descending upon a light, as you breathe 'Hu' back down your spine. Experience the state of Islam – the state of total surrender to the grace of the One Beloved.

63

MEDITATION 24
WORKING WITH YOUR CORE MANTRA

**One mantra used every day, for many years, cannot
fail to open the inner doorway.**

It is important, in today's ever shrinking world, to acknowledge the
shared origin of all the world's spiritual traditions. At the same
time, our practice should not be too shallow. We need to dig at least
one well, very deeply, so that we gain access to the hidden stream
of joyful awareness, underlying all spiritual traditions. This is the
narrow path of one mantra, the core practise to which we feel
especially drawn. At the right time, the right heart practice will find
you. It will uplift you, and test you, ease your struggle, and cause
you to struggle. It will demand commitment, and help you to let go,
refine the mind, and open the heart. Ideally you will practise one
mantra, every day, morning and evening.

CORE METHOD

1. Repeat your chosen mantra out loud, feeling and hearing the
sound vibration, reverberating in your being.
2. Continue repeating the mantra silently in your heart, feeling its
presence.
3. Stop repetition and become absorbed in the presence.
4. Remember your source in being.

USING MANTRA AND BREATH

Synchronise your silent mantra repetition with your breathing.
Repeat your mantra as you breathe in, and repeat your mantra as
you breathe out. Imagine you are breathing your mantra in, and out,
of the very cells of your body. With the mantra flowing on the
current of your breath, it is very close to your heart. Focus on your
heart, as you breathe your mantra in, and out, and imagine you are
breathing your mantra in, and out, of your heart centre. Now
practise the suspension of your breath a few times, without
straining, and keep repeating the mantra, in the space between your
breaths, still focusing on your heart centre. This exercise adds focus
and vitality very quickly to your mantra practise. But do not get too
attached to your breathing, or centres in your body. Return to
simple, devotional, repetition, without location or focus on breath.
As your mantra practice warms up, it becomes your sole reality. It is
no longer in you. You are in your mantra, and your mantra carries
you back to the presence and being of God.

STAGE SEVEN

ABSORBED IN PRESENCE MEDITATION

Tomb of one of the sons of 'Akbar the Great', who died believing in the unity of the worlds religions. A place of great presence.

YOGIC WORD - DHYANA

With your eyes, you can see what is in front of you. With your ears, you can hear greater distances. With your heart, you can feel the heart-beat of your beloved a thousand miles away. Try just sitting and feeling the presence, in and around you, until your heart truly awakens.

Repeating the mantra, we start to experience the sound of the sound. We feel the vibration that the mantra carries, the presence of God that the mantra brings. This is the fruit of the meditation. Having knocked at the door, there comes a moment when we stop knocking and allow the door to open. Grace takes over from personal effort. We stop speaking and start listening. We progress from the dimension of sound to the dimension of feeling. If we close our eyes and block our ears, our sensation of feeling remains. This sense is attuned not to the eyes or the ears, but the heart. This sensation of feeling in our heart brings us close to the direct experience of God. We travel from our head centre to our heart centre. We feel lifted up into the presence of love, or truth, or joy, whichever our mantra brings, and our heart opens and starts to sing. We become absorbed in the object of our meditation and go with the flow. Anyone who has got lost in gardening, cooking, painting or loving knows this experience. It is the difference between thinking about an idea, and living the reality on all levels of our being. In yogic terms this is when we move from concentration, 'Dharana', to meditation, 'Dhyana'. We travel from doctrines which divide, to love which unites.

The practise of letting go of the mantra is important. Mantra is a concentration on a small point. Repeating the mantra, we walk down the straight and narrow path. But when we arrive at our destination, the view broadens. We feel the expansiveness of the heart, the presence of One Being, a vibration of spiritual feeling that radiates out from our being. As we become advanced in meditation, we realise that this vibration is the goal of meditation. In fact, this presence is the secret of unceasing prayer, whilst living a normal life. We can talk about mundane things and radiate love at the same time. This is the Holy Spirit we seek and in which we love to live. Soon we can attune to this feeling in minutes and even seconds. We realise this presence is available to us in all places and at all times with a small inner adjustment of awareness. Just as it takes great heat to boil cold water, the heat of our spiritual struggle, through mantra, raises our vibration. Once we are boiling we can turn the heat down and just keep things simmering. We can live a normal life and remember our sacred origins. Every experience becomes richer, multi-textured and multi-dimensional.

BUDDHA

'For greater than all the joys of heaven and earth, greater still than dominion over all the worlds, is the joy of reaching the stream.'

JESUS

'Whoever drinks of the water that I shall give him will never thirst; the water that I shall give him will become in him a spring of water welling up to eternal life.'

'God is spirit, and those who worship him must worship in spirit and truth.'

ST PAUL TO THE CORINTHIANS

'We teach what scripture calls: the things that no eye has seen and no ear has heard, things beyond the mind of man, all that God has prepared for those who love him. These are the very things that God has revealed to us through the Spirit, for the Spirit reaches the depths of everything, even the depths of God.'

ST SYMEON THE NEW THEOLOGIAN

'There is a fourth rung or stage in the spiritual life - that of the old man with grey hairs. This signifies undeviating absorption in contemplation, and this is the state of the perfect.'

UPANISHADS

'Meditate and realise this world is filled with the presence of God.'

RUMI

'I'm stubborn, ecstatic and nosy; my friend so delicate, impatient and weary. Without a messenger between us how can we find harmony? We can only meet in God's presence.'

PATANJALI

'A steady, continuous flow of attention directed towards the same point or region is meditation (Dhyana).'

MEDITATION 25
FACILITATING HEART FEELING – 9 PRACTISES

There is a saying, that when the heart awakens, we are known by our silence, our laughter and our tears. These are the signs of profound feeling. These are the clues that our heart has awoken. Here are some practises to help you get in touch with your feeling centre.

BECOME THE MUSIC

Sit in meditation posture, in your place of meditation. Put on some calming, uplifting music. This is not background music. This is the object of your total focus and concentration. Listen to the music with all your heart. Become absorbed in the music. Let the music carry you away. Let the sound change your mood, loosen you up, lift your feeling and move your heart and soul.

ENERGY FLOWING BETWEEN THE HANDS

Breathe deep into your abdomen and out of your heart. Imagine you are breathing light, from the Cosmos, deep into your core, and then back up and out again, radiating out from your heart centre. Hold your hands in front of you - palms facing each other and apart. Breathing in, draw your hands apart and breathing out, draw your hands closer together. Feel the energy between your hands becoming stronger as the hands get closer. Feel the energy, and visualize light, travelling between your hands. The light flowing out of your heart centre is flowing down your arms and between your hands. Use this flowing practise to increase the feeling of presence in your hands, heart and around your body.

3 HEART SYMBOLS

This meditation connects us to three different dimensions of the heart centre. First attune to your human heart, on the left side, visualizing a red rose. Breathe in the Arabic wazifa 'Ya Rahman' – the warm merciful love of God. Feel the soft tissues of your human heart being bathed in, and radiating, the warm sun-like love of the Creator. Now attune to your spiritual heart, on the right side of your chest – the 'Guha' - the centre meditated on by mystics of all traditions. Visualize a white rose representing the purity of spirit. Breathe in the wazifa 'Ya Rahim' – the spiritual compassion of the One. Feel the cooler, purified love represented by the moon. Focus now on your heart chakra, in the centre of your chest, visualizing a golden rose. Repeat the wazifa 'Ya Khabir' – the all knowing heart.

THE SPACE IN THE CAVE OF MY HEART

Sitting still, focus on your heart, as you breathe in and out. Visualize your heart centre as a cave. A safe, sacred space protected by cave walls. Enter the cave space in your heart centre. Light a candle of warmth, inspiration and love in the cave of your heart centre. Retreat to your cave whenever you feel you need more inner light. Nobody can enter the cave without your permission. Nobody can take the space in your heart centre away from you. Whatever your predicament, whatever your circumstances, you can always retreat to the space and candle light, in the cave of your heart.

A BEAUTIFUL FLOWER UNFOLDING

Breathing in and out of your heart, imagine that your heart is a flower. Let your feeling centre, your intuition, choose the flower. Choose the specimen and the colour. Visualize your flower, depicting the tenderness, beauty and harmony of your innermost centre, in every detail. As you breathe in, allow the light of the Cosmos to bathe your heart flower in life-sustaining energy. As you breathe out, witness the petals opening and unfolding. Smell the perfume of your flower, as you visualize the beautiful qualities of your innermost being, manifesting in your life.

MINDFULNESS MEDITATION

Many Buddhist meditations bring us to full awareness in the present moment. These 'mindfulness' meditations are not designed to destroy our creative imagination, or to reduce the unlimited richness of life into a bland, one-dimensional reality. They take us through the doorway of the present moment into the boundless realm of eternity. From the one-track thinking of the head, into the multi-dimensional feeling of the heart. From the sleep state of doing one thing and thinking another, to the awakened state where every action is a revelation of the mystery of life. Whilst washing the dishes, repeat to yourself, 'I am washing the dishes in order to wash the dishes'. See your dishwashing as an end in itself, your sole purpose in life. Enter fully into every sensation of the dishwashing experience. Give yourself fully, on every level, to this practise of dishwashing. You are washing your soul, serving your body and those around you, restoring order in the universe, meditating on the cleansing qualities of water, connecting to the lives of those who made the plates and ate off the plates. This is heart centred dishwashing.

WALKING WITH PRESENCE

Find a quiet place to walk, preferably in nature and preferably in solitude. You can practise this with shoes, or even better, without. Assume an upright posture and breathe deep into your abdomen. Step forward, leading with your solar plexus, with your chest and attitude open and expansive. Move as slowly as you possibly can. Feel every aspect of your movement as intensely as you can, and every sensation in your body as sensitively as you can. This slow movement with presence creates an enhanced awareness of all the dimensions of your being. Enjoy being, in the midst of movement.

SITTING IN A CAFÉ

We need to find ways to harmonise with the circumstances of our times. Cafes are ideal places to practise being and presence, in the rush around conditions of our materialistic society. Hold your chosen drink between the palms of your hands and treasure every sensation. Be grateful for this opportunity to sit still, the convivial ambience of your surroundings, the holiday atmosphere as people take a break. Breathe deeply. Slowly enjoy your beverage, revelling in every sensation and nuance of this pleasurable experience. Sit with great presence, looking completely normal in the middle of the crowd, experiencing deeply and keeping your outer awareness.

TWIRLING WITH MUSIC

Find some beautiful heart/soul stirring music without a jarring rhythm. Stand up and place your left hand on your heart, and your right hand on your left hand, nurturing and stimulating your heart centre. As the music plays, slowly begin to rotate towards your left side, flowing with the emotion of the music. Slowly unfurl your right arm and hand upwards, palm face up, as if gathering energy from above. At the same time unfurl your left arm and hand downwards, palm down. Your arms now form a continuous conduit, receiving energy from above, through your right palm, flowing through your heart, and flowing out of your left palm. As you continue to rotate, slowly bring your hands back into your heart and then unfurl them again continuously, as you feel moved, in harmony with the music and your inner rhythm. This beautiful twirling meditation evokes the circular motion of the planets, mingled with the emotion and rhythm of your heart.

STAGE EIGHT

LOST IN THE ONE
SUBJECT BECOMES OBJECT

Sunset on the Baltic

YOGIC WORD
NIRVIKALPA SAMADHI

Everyone is looking for unity. Nobody likes division, conflict and separation. Deep down, we all sense that we have a common source and that the dualities of this world are a veil, obscuring reality. Whether through the path of love, or truthfulness, or peace, we all want to come home.

Downplaying the movements of our body and mind in meditation, we discover that our life force increases. We realise that we are more than a tiny body and mind, with its limited vantage point. The 'I' gets dislodged from its identity with this particular body and mind, and discovers its true mooring in spirit, presence, love and being. We live from the heart, rather than the head. Our sense of self expands from the small body/mind ego to the Universal being, behind the appearance of things. We move according to the pulse of the creator, echoed in the universe, echoed in our heart centre. We come to realise that we are a soul incarnated in a body, not a body trying to be a soul. We are the One Spirit, formed into a soul, not a soul trying to remember its source. We experience ourselves as a wave arising out of the sea of Divine Consciousness. This can happen as a sudden experience, or slowly and steadily, over many years of spiritual practise, like water wearing down a hard stone.

The process of transforming our very identity doesn't ever stop. There are ever wider ways of communing with this mysterious reality called Life. Life has a dynamic element that keeps moving on. Whenever we think we have reached the summit, a new horizon appears. Whenever we think we know, we discover that we don't. Jesus said that only God knows when the end of times will be. We all have to surrender to the Mystery, as in 'Islam'-'submission'.

In Christianity, this realisation is called being 'Born Again' in the Spirit, realising that we are children of God. In Buddhism this experience is called 'Enlightenment'. In Hinduism this experience is called 'Self-Realisation' or 'God-Consciousness'. In Islam this experience is called 'Fana', extinction in Allah. In Yoga this experience is called 'Nirvikalpa Samadhi'. In psychological terms, we identify with the larger 'Self', rather than the ego.

When we experience a new revelation about who we are, the experience never leaves us. We may not always experience the same bliss, as the first moment that a new vista in our being opens out, but we can never forget. Our psyche relaxes. We may discover that this body and mind, which we have called 'me', is simply the clothing we are wearing, and that this world is a stage on which our body acts its part. We are beyond and set free by the Truth. We may re-discover ourselves at the Heart of All, born again of the spirit in deep communion, recognizing the 'Other' as our very self.

BUDDHA

'Understand that the body is merely the foam of a wave, the shadow of a shadow. Snap the flower arrows of desire and then, unseen, escape the king of death.'

'You are the lamp to lighten the way. Then hurry, hurry. When your light shines purely you will not be born and you will not die.'

'All things arise and pass away. But the awakened awake forever.'

JESUS

'Truly, truly I say to you unless one is born of water and the Spirit, he cannot enter the Kingdom of God. That which is born of flesh is flesh, and that which is born of the Spirit is spirit.'

'Truly, truly I say to you, unless a grain of wheat falls into the earth and dies, it remains alone; but if it dies, it bears much fruit.'

'You are the light of the world.'

KRISHNA

'There the sun shines not, nor the moon gives light, nor fire burns, for the Light of my glory is there. Those who reach that abode return no more.'

'A spark of my eternal spirit becomes in this world a living soul.'

'Beginningless and free from changing conditions, imperishable is the Spirit Supreme. Though he is in the body, not his is the work of the body, and he is pure from the imperfection of all work.'

RUMI

'Die! Die! Die in this love! If you die in this love your soul will be renewed.'

PATANJALI

'When the object of meditation engulfs the meditator, appearing as the subject, self-awareness is lost. This is Samadhi.'

MEDITATION 26
SELF-ENQUIRY. WHO AM I?

This meditation focuses our awareness back onto its source, looking within and asking 'but who am I in the first place?' It's strange to think that the one constant in our life, our self, is in fact a mystery!

As you sit in meditation, ask yourself 'Am I my body?' As soon as you say 'my body' you are acknowledging that your body is a possession and not actually you. When you sleep and have no use of your body, you are still aware of existing. When you sit in meditation with eyes closed in silence, body motionless, you are still aware of a strong feeling of being alive. You have to conclude 'I am not simply my body'. Now ask 'Am I my mind?' 'Am I my thoughts?' As soon as you say 'my thoughts' you are admitting that you 'have' thoughts – that there is a 'you' before there is a thought. How is it that you witness your thoughts? Your thoughts come and go, but there is still a 'you', watching your thoughts. Between every thought, there is a space. You do not cease to exist in that space. In fact the bigger space there is between your thoughts, the stronger the feeling of being alive. You have to conclude 'I am not my thoughts'. Now you may ask 'Perhaps I am my personality, my character?' When you analyse it, it becomes clear that your personality only exists in flow, in self expression, in movement. In stillness, in silence, you have no personality and no character, but you still exist. You have to conclude. 'I am not just my personality'. You can then ask 'Am I my consciousness, am I my awareness, am I perhaps, the one that witnesses all the movements of my life?' You have to admit, that in all the movements and stillness of your life, your awareness is unbroken. There is always an awareness witnessing your life. But do you own that awareness? Is it yours?

The key breakthrough in meditation is when we realise that the awareness is not 'ours'. The body/mind complex, called the 'ego', has a tendency to lay claim to the awareness that flows through it, effectively taking God prisoner. As we meditate more on awareness, we realise that there is only one awareness - the One awareness that 'owns' our body/mind. It is the same awareness that lights up our neighbour's eyes, the One Being who becomes us. We are waves arising out of the sea of consciousness. In India, this ocean is called,'Sat-Chit-Ananda' – Being, Consciousness, Bliss. There is but One Being, and one ocean, with many emerging waves.

This sacred mountain in Tamil Nadu is called Arunachala. It is
the sacred hill that inspired the great 20th Century India sage
Sri Ramana Maharshi. Spending 17 years meditating in one of
the hills caves, Sri Ramana eventually became the focal point of
an Ashram at the foot of the hill, where he taught people to
enquire into their very nature. Teaching the way of Self-
Enquiry he radiated truth, love and peace to all-comers.

"The sage is characterized by eternal and intense activity.
His stillness is like the apparent stillness of a fast rotating
top. Its very speed cannot be followed by the eye and so it
appears to be still. Yet it is rotating. So is the apparent
inaction of the sage. People mistake stillness for inertness. It
is not so."- Sri Ramana Maharshi

MEDITATION 27
BECOMING THE WITNESS

Sit still and just watch your thoughts. Don't follow them. Don't lose yourself in them. Just watch. Imagine you are a cat stalking your prey. Sit still, poised, for the next thought to come along. Don't follow the thought. Watch and remain awake, alert, and attentive.

Between your thoughts is a space. From that space, you are watching your thoughts. If there was no space, there would be no place from which to watch your thoughts. If you are watching your thoughts, then 'you' cannot be your thoughts. You are not limited by your thoughts. You must exist independent of your thoughts. You must be in that space from which you are watching your thoughts. As you watch your thoughts, without judging and without identifying, you are becoming the witness. You are connecting to your unlimited potential in the source. Imagine you are God. Imagine you are an impartial observer of your thoughts. Imagine you are from another planet. Realise that your thoughts are simply a product of a particular body/mind matrix, occurring in a particular time and place. See that the one thinking, the one watching, the one upon whose screen the thoughts are playing, is unconditioned and unaffected by the events of life. Think of the times, you have blamed your bad actions, on the way you have been conditioned by peoples' bad treatment of you. Realise that you are only bound by your past, so long as you remain stuck in your thoughts. See how stepping into the space between your thoughts, you enter the present moment, become free, and access the point of unlimited creativity in the 'now'. Imagine your life is a play. Connecting to the space between your thoughts, realise that your unconditioned Self can create any thoughts and write any script it wishes. See how these thoughts become the actions, and how these actions cause the reactions, that become your destiny. See how you are both the creator and witness of your life. Develop the ability to detach your identification of who you are, from your thoughts. Develop the skill of simply watching the thoughts, as they arise and fall, and come and go, like clouds in the sky. Identify for once with the sky, and not the clouds. Identify for once with the witness, and not the witnessed. Identify for once with the thinker, and not the thoughts, and become aware of your unlimited freedom in being.

MEDITATION 28
FREEDOM IN SPACE

Most of our lives we concentrate on form. We identify ourselves with our body, and the thought forms we create in our head. We move forward in life, towards dream objects we create in our minds. Our security is based on attaching our form, who we think we are, to forms around us. No form can exist without space. All forms go through a cycle which ends in destruction. Is life then to be found in form? Do forms really exist or do they only appear to exist as separate entities. Does life simply use different forms to express its inexhaustible essence? Think of how water flows into many different forms and assumes different shapes, but is really shapeless life-giving flow. Think of how notes become music by their invisible arrangement and rhythm, which expresses something we feel but can't see. Matter is, in fact, mostly space. Every atom, according to science, consists of tiny electrons circling a nucleus, but mostly space. According to modern physics, the universe is largely invisible, dark matter. Behind matter is anti-matter. For objects to move they need space to flow in.

Look at an object in front of you. Now instead of looking at the object, look at the space that the object is placed in. Concentrate on the space that holds the object. Now become aware of the object that holds that space - maybe the room. Now become aware of the space that the room is occupying - maybe the house. Close your eyes. Keep your awareness on that space. Keep expanding your awareness to encompass bigger objects, and bigger spaces. Let your awareness of space expand to a cosmic scale. Now become aware that this concentration has silenced your thoughts. Realise that, for a moment, you have entered the space between your thoughts. From this space, all thoughts emerge and back into this space, all thoughts merge. Feel, in this space, the presence of being that is pure consciousness, unrestricted by a particular idea or form. The longer you can remain in the space between your thoughts, the stronger you will experience the enlivening presence of pure consciousness. Become aware, that all problems are contained by a bigger space. There is always a beginning and an end to a problem. Like clouds in the sky, problems come and go, but the backdrop, the formless sky, always remains. Whatever horizon you are aiming at, remember you can always take the horizon away and going nowhere, be free.

MEDITATION 29
DYING TO THE SMALL SELF

Self-Realisation is a process of identifying with the eternal Self and letting go of the limited self. That, which the Hindu tradition calls the 'Self', the Western tradition calls 'God'. That, which the Western tradition calls the 'Sinner', the Eastern tradition calls the 'ego'. The Self is the One Being, discovered from the inside out. God is the One Being, discovered from the outside in. These two practises help us discover the One from both directions.

FROM SUFI TRADITION

Sit in kneeling position. Bow forward, breathing out, and repeat the words 'I die in you'. As you repeat these words, feel yourself letting go of your limited, mind/body self-identification. Breathing in, sit back up, repeating the words: 'I rise in you'. As you repeat these words, identify with the One Being, whom you really are, rising up within you. Each time you bow forward, breathing out, die to your ego. Each time you sit up again, breathing in, feel reborn in spirit - your true Self. Each time you bow forward, place your limited self in the hands of God – the Universal Self. Each time your body rises, feel Gods love lifting your body.

FROM CHRISTIAN TRADITION

Repeat the same movements and breathing, but now as you bow forward, repeat the Christian mantra 'Kyrie Eleison'. As you sit back up, repeat the words 'Christie Eleison'. Each time you bow forward, breathing out, let go of all your limitations and weaknesses into the hands of the One Lord - the One Being of Love. Surrender. As you sit back up, feel the grace of the One Being, pouring into you, recreating you. Emerge, as a wave rising up from the ocean. As you bow forward, lay down your life. As you sit back up, feel the grace of spirit resurrecting you. As you bow forward, you become Christ. As you sit up, Christ becomes you. As you bow forward, appeal to God for mercy, with all you heart. As you sit up, feel Christ rising within you, in answer to your prayer.

STAGE NINE

SURRENDER IN LOVE
EYES OPEN MEDITATION

A happy couple stroll in Delhi

The Garden of Gethsemane – 'Thy will be done'

YOGIC WORD – SAHAJA SAMADHI

FINDING OUR PURPOSE IN LIFE

In the final stage of meditation, we come back down the mountain. Having stepped off the world for a moment, we now help the world move forward, and we are known by our fruits. Having realised who we are beyond this world, we now realise who we are within the world. Set free by the Truth, we learn to embrace limitation again, for the purposes of Love. We realise the love purpose of creation itself - the One sacrificing or dividing itself into the Many, so that the Many can rediscover the One. We now learn to love God in our fellow human beings. In Yoga this is called 'Sahaja Samadhi'. Eyes open meditation – the permanent state. We surrender to the dynamic mystery of life's continuing unfoldment. We see the 'One' in the 'Many'. Having discovered the Creator in stillness, we now rediscover the Creator in movement. We work to fulfil the purpose of creation, to bring heaven on earth, and help build a beautiful world, full of beautiful people. We don't see the world and our ego as an illusion. We realize that they are the funnelled down expression of the Creators Divine Love, expressing itself in creative, mysterious and beautiful ways. We actually become Co-Creators, dancing with the Divine in love. We see even our weaknesses, flaws and idiosyncrasies as variations on the Divine Theme, and we passionately work to fulfil our purposes in life, as perfectly as we can. The God, whom we previously worshipped as 'One', we now see manifesting as 'Three' - a dynamic Trinity in Being. The divine in-breath towards the 'One' emerges as a divine out-breath, revealing the 'Three'. In Buddhism, neither the Thinker, the Thought nor the act of Thinking, are not the One. In Hinduism, the Divine is seen as Brahma, the Creator, Vishnu, the Preserver, and Siva, the Destroyer, as well as being beyond all three. In Christianity, the One God moves as three – Father, Son and Holy Spirit.

In this final stage we go through the process of recreating our life, actions, habits and even personality to reflect the love at the heart of our being, as does a Saint or Master. We rediscover the details of life as sacred, rather than just irrelevant. We return to a normal life, but now see the extra-ordinary at the heart of the ordinary. We return to our jobs and families, but now we carry with us a deeper love, and greater insight. We meditate to help the world and we see, in our neighbours eyes, the One Beloved, our very Self.

80

BUDDHA
'Your work is to discover your work, and then with all your heart, to give yourself to it.'
'In this world hate never yet dispelled hate. Only love dispels hate. This is the law, ancient and inexhaustible.'
'The fool laughs at generosity. The miser cannot enter heaven. But the master finds joy in giving and happiness is his reward.'

JESUS
'As you did it to one of the least of these my brethren, you did it to me.'
'Love one another as I have loved you. Greater love has no man than this, that a man lay down his life for his friends.'
'I send you out as sheep in the midst of wolves; so be wise as serpents and innocent as doves.'

KRISHNA
'He who sees that the Lord of All is ever the same in all that is - immortal in the field of mortality-he sees the truth. And when a man sees that the God in himself is the same God in all that is, he hurts not himself by hurting others; then he goes indeed to the highest Path.'
'Only by love can men see me, and know me, and come to me.'

RUMI
'If you have illusions about heaven lose them. The soul heard of one attribute of Love and came to earth. A hundred attributes of heaven could never charm her back. It is here the soul discovers the reality of love.'

LAO TZU
'To the good I would be good; to the not-good I would also be good, in order to make them good.'

KORAN
'In the Name of God, the merciful, the compassionate.'

MEDITATION 30
SUNLIGHT DANCING ON BROKEN WATER

Imagine a lake of water rippling in the wind. See how the waves distort and break the images reflected in the lake. Imagine now the sunlight shining on the waters surface. See how the waves cause the sunlight to dance and sparkle in a beautiful way.

Reflect for a moment on how the brokenness of our humanity, the idiosyncrasies and weaknesses of our nature can become a source of beauty, in the light of our souls. See how our breakdowns sometimes move us onto new and greater horizons, on our journey through life. See how the fragility of our hearts gives us access to a profoundly touching dimension of reality, which adds purpose and meaning to our lives, just as a crackly record can sometimes be more beautiful than a flawless one. Realise how our flaws become the questions which determine the direction of our soul's journey through this world, in search of an answer.

Allow yourself to open for a moment to your inner wounds, brokenness, crucifixions and disappointments. Don't use your head too much. Follow your intuition and heart. Let go of the masks holding in your inner pain. Don't run away from your suffering and don't cling to it. Rather, hold your inner tragedy in the loving embrace and light of your immaculate soul. Think of someone who you love unconditionally, or who loves you unconditionally. Reconnect to that feeling of unconditional love. Hold your inner suffering in the warmth and tenderness of that unconditional acceptance and understanding. Feel yourself healing, letting go and releasing. Allow your Resurrection to happen, through the grace of the One Being of Love. The secret of this meditation is in the mingling of our wholeness and our brokenness. Accepting our brokenness, in an embrace of unconditional love, from the heart, we melt and mold ourselves into a more beautiful being.

In Islam it is believed that our soul borrows a personality made of the fabric of matter, so as to improve it, and hand it over to another incoming soul, on leaving the earth. Imagine your purpose in life is not just to become free, but to recreate your personality in more beautiful ways. Visualize how you would like to behave. Bathing in the light of your soul, visualize your personality changing into a more beautiful creation, contributing more to creating a beautiful world full of beautiful people.

MEDITATION 31
LIGHT DESCENDING – A LIGHT UPON A LIGHT

Travel up your spine, through the colour spectrum, as in meditation 12. Imagine you travel up and out the top of your skull. Let go, for a second, into the eternal, formless, black light of space. Your prayer of light is flying heavenwards. In the moment between your in-breath and out-breath, the Holy Spirit will emerge, as at Pentecost.

Like a new, brilliant, white star born out of a black hole, feel the descent of a brilliant, white light. As a light descending upon a light, feel the white light, which contains within it all light, descending through the top of your skull. You are now in a state of total surrender and receptiveness.

Feel the light entering your third eye. See the cosmos with God's eyes. Opening your eyes, focus on something. Realize that the light of the One Being is looking at creation through your eyes. Feel the light of God, uplifting and rejuvenating the object in view. Feel the white light descend to the throat centre. See how your life story expresses variations on the one cosmic drama of unfolding humanity. See how your life is the tip of the iceberg. How you are a small part in the eternal dance, between the forces of action and reaction, light and dark, pleasure and pain. You are an actor in the great divine drama. Feel the white light descend to your heart centre. Feel how the One Light can work through you to reach out to all, in love. Through your arms, smiles, emotion, warmth and joy the One Being is intimately embracing creation. Feel the white light descend to your solar plexus. See how the One Light, can give birth to new forms, embodied in your actions. Feel how divine seeds, rise through the collective unconscious, which Jung spoke about, entering your personal unconscious in creative ideas and inspirations. Feel the white light descend to the sexual area. Feel the intimacy of the Divine, as it expresses itself, through pleasure, the intense belonging of family relationships and the bringing of souls into new bodies. The Divine wants to be felt and touched. Feel the white light descend to your base chakra, reconnecting to the earth. Feel how the mystery of our lives is framed by the mystery of the relationship between our Father in Heaven and Mother Earth, and how we are all children of both, while we live on earth. As the One Father Light descends into Mother Earth, the Divine Alchemy continues to create heaven on earth, starting with nature and moving on to animals and humans.

MEDITATION 32
DEEPER, WIDER, HIGHER

Meditation is always about going further. Expanding, deepening, and heightening our experience. It is never about switching off and experiencing nothing. It is about refining our sensitivity, broadening our horizons and raising our consciousness. We rise above and beyond, dive deep within, and reach out further and further, according to the ebb and flow of the moment. When we reach the place of 'no-thing', we are then in the place of full potentiality, rather than the place of great slumber! In India they call the state of sleep 'Tamasic', the state of activity 'Rajasic' and the state of serenity 'Sattvic'. The place we aim for in meditation is 'Sattvic' - the highest fulfilment. This becomes the stepping off point for the experience of unity. We switch on, until there is nothing left to switch on, then the All can finally become us, through the space created in our heart and we realise our eternal dimension in being.

As you sit in meditation, breathing into your abdomen, feel ever profounder dimensions of peace, as you reach deep within. Go further, into deeper and deeper zones of reality, letting go of more and more.

As you sit in meditation, breathing up and down your spine, feel ever greater heights of truth and clarity, as you reach up and beyond the conditions of your life. Feel that your vision is becoming crystal clear, sharp and penetrating, illuminated by heavenly light.

As you sit in meditation, breathing the Cosmos in and out of your Heart, feel ever more tender and expansive waves of love, as you reach out to the world, cosmos and Creator - more romantic than Romeo and Juliet, more tender than the sweetest love making, more understanding than the greatest counsellor.

Truly speaking the spiritual journey has no end, so long as life itself has no end. If you think you've arrived, you haven't - you've just stopped growing. If you think you're enlightened, you've accepted a limited idea of what enlightenment is. As the Zen teacher T.D Suzuki said, strictly speaking, there are no enlightened beings, only enlightened moments and we move from one enlightened moment to the next, in this wonderful mystery called life - beyond the beyond, as the Buddha said, becoming perfect as the Father in heaven is perfect, as Jesus said.

MEDITATION 33
LOVE IN ACTION

If love is the culmination of a profound journey into Truth and Being, our actions of compassion will be surrounded by the aura of profound peace. They will be spontaneous and joyful, from the depths, height and width of our being. The secret of meditation, is that by leading us into an experience of unity, it becomes our nature to love, to be truthful and to rest in peace. All three qualities will be present and balanced in our actions. Meditation teaches us both how to stop causing suffering in life, and how to embrace life with love.

HEART QUESTIONING

Sit quietly, and ask your heart these questions. Allow the answers to arise spontaneously from within. You can try this exercise with a partner, asking your partner to read out the question and then give a heart felt answer. You can ask the questions just before going to sleep, asking your Heart to reveal to you an answer in your dreams. Ask each question three times. Try to go deeper into the question each time, peeling off your protective layers, diving within.

HEART, what does the universe ask of me in this life?

HEART, what dream is unfulfilled in my life?

HEART, whom do I love and serve in this life?

HEART, where are you in my life?

HEART FELT ACTIONS

Follow up on the answers you have received, putting your love into action. If you feel like it, try some of these suggestions: Learn to dance. Learn to sing. Cook a beautiful meal for a new person. Do something lovely for someone you don't like. Face a challenge that frightens you. Clean your home with love and make it more beautiful. Spend a long time talking to someone who did not interest you before. Create something, from nothing, that will last. Make a sacrifice of love for someone and see what happens. Spend a day smiling at strangers. Take the time to talk to anyone who serves you in life. Commit yourself to a new good cause, beyond immediate concerns. Make peace with everyone in your life. Change a habit, for the health and happiness of your body. Perfect a new skill, or a talent. Receiving from within, give to people around you, without expectation of return.

MEDITATION 34
ZIKR – MEDITATION IN MOTION

This form of Sufi meditation is usually practised in kneeling posture. It can be practised in sitting posture if kneeling doesn't agree with your knees. The following concentration is one from many that can be practised with Zikr, balancing the three qualities of Truth, Love and Peace in our energy field. The experience we get from Zikr is more embodied than the experience we get from sitting in lotus posture. We may experience our very atoms awakening.

There are three movements to the Zikr. First is a circle, breathing out, rotating the spine to the left, then forward, then to right, then back up. The head turns to the left shoulder, down and to the front, to the right shoulder, and returns to the centre, looking up. This spiralling of the body evokes the rotation of spirit, moving in life. It can represent the ascent or the descent of spirit, into or out of matter, depending on the experience. Repeat the Wazifa 'Ya Haqq', as you circle round. Feel the vibration of Truth, as it manifests in the movement of your life, in ascending circles of aspiration. Travel from the release of authenticity, feeling where you are, good and bad, right now, to the experience of the One Truth beyond all, as you circle upwards. Feel, as you spiral around, that you are releasing toxins, and impurities out in all directions, and raising your vibration upwards, as you spiral up, towards the One Being.

The second movement is a forward and downward plunge, bringing the body forward, followed by an upward ascent, returning your spine to straight and your head to looking upwards. This represents the journeys of incarnation and ascension. Breathe in, as you trace this line down and up. Repeat the Wazifa "Ya Waduud" – the give and take of love. Feel yourself travelling deep within, and then aspiring very high, with the vibration of love. Feel the descent of love and grace as you bend down, and feel the surge of new love and creativity born from within matter, as you rise back up.

In the final movement, we keep the spine straight and slightly turn the head to the left hand side, breathing out, into the natural heart centre. We connect, in this movement, to what it means to be a complete human being, bringing together the vertical and horizontal dimensions of our being. Repeat "Ya Salaam", experiencing peace beyond understanding, descending and radiating out, through all of the pores and atoms of your body.

MEDITATION 35
INVOKING THE THIRD FORCE

The final stage of meditation is all about making a difference. In the same way that a 'Saviour' actually intervenes in peoples lives, or a 'Bodhisattva' delays his or her own enlightenment, for the sake of everyone else, or an advanced yogi 'takes' the karma of a disciple, we are interested in transforming, not just escaping from, matter. This is the deep meaning of the word 'Resurrection'. Matter is actually re-constituted in a spiritual format. The physical body becomes a spiritual body. The universe actually has a creative purpose. Something meaningful and creative actually happens.

Very often, in our lives, we get stuck. We see two options. If we turn left, we get half of what we want, but we can't bear the consequences. And the same if we turn right. For example, maybe we hate our job, but we can't pay for our house doing a job we love. Maybe, we are willing to sell our house, but the housing market has collapsed, or our partner will leave us. This is when we need to invoke the third force. We need to move from the world of the 'two' to the world of the 'three'. Of course, we can become absorbed in the One and forget our problems, but our situation may not change. If however, we can appeal to the One, as a third force, in the midst of our problems, either our situation or our perception of our situation, can be transformed.

This is common in all spiritual traditions. Traditionally it is called, 'talking to God.' When God is described as Mother, Father and Son, the Son is often called upon to solve our problems. In Hinduism, Ganesh, the elephant-headed son of Siva and Parvati, is invoked to overcome obstacles, and their second son, Muruga, wins battles. In the Christian Trinity, the Holy Spirit is invoked to get things moving, and to change the context of our problems. Looking at the human body we can invoke the Heart for assistance. Between our difficult situation, and our ideal dreams, we can call upon the Divine Assistance to bring about a transformation, a miracle.

Look at a place in your life that is stuck between two opposites. Hold those two opposites in your heart, and appeal to your chosen third force, to transform matters, for the highest good of all. Now let go of the problem, and trust that a resolution, or even re-evaluation of your situation, will emerge. Stay awake, because your prayer will be answered, although rarely as you expect!

MEDITATION 36
SINGING YOUR SONG, DANCING YOUR DANCE

As you have progressed through this course, you may have found some practices helpful, and others, not so. You may have discovered a particular affinity with one tradition, several or none. You may be working with a spiritual community, guide or none. The key point is to develop your heart practise - your core path. No two paths are the same. No book or system contains all your answers. The answers are within you, depending on the questions that your particular vocation in life, evoke. The path is made of many small steps. Right now, only one step - this step. Once you move forward on the spiritual path, the One Being comes running to meet you. Once you begin to knock, doors begin to open. Trust in the process. There are no accidents on the spiritual path. God, your Heart, your very Self, is leading you home, inspiring you to practise meditation.

Aged 33, Jesus allowed himself to be taken from his disciples for the first time. There is a time on the spiritual path when the teacher disappears. On his deathbed, Buddha is said to have exhorted his disciples to make of themselves a light and to rely on no-one else. There is a point on the spiritual journey when we must look within and find our own Realisation. As George Fox, the founder of Quakerism, often asked, whatever the scriptures may say, what have you discovered in your life? Hazrat Inayat Khan, the founder of the Sufi Order, said we progress on our spiritual journey from being deer - always running in a herd to a quiet and sheltered spot, to being lions - bravely facing alone, if necessary, all the challenges that life throws at us. We could say that we progress from being children, following and taking orders, to being adults, being creative in our own right, with our own song to sing. When we are children, we rely on our parents. When we are students, we rely on our teacher. When we are adults, we rely on God alone. The methods of meditation we have used, finally melt into moments of spontaneous meaningfulness, beyond description. And when we come to describe our experience, we will frame it in our own unique way. We may choose to worship, work and live within many different communities but we all have our personal relationship and reckoning with the One Being, who is our source, inspiration, and ultimate love.

PART 1V
THE PROCESS

40 WAYS TO EARMARK THE SPIRITUAL JOURNEY IN 3 SIMPLE STEPS

A Saint meditating on a 'Yoni Lingam' (male/female symbol) in India

"Before I had studied Zen, I saw mountains as mountains, waters as waters. When I learned something of Zen, the mountains were no longer mountains, waters no longer waters. But now that I understand Zen, I am a peace with myself, seeing mountains once again as mountains, waters as waters."

Chinese Master Ch-Ing-Yuan (660-740)

Meditation acts as a catalyst, speeding up the evolution of consciousness. It helps us move towards, rather than away from, the One Light. Simplifying the process into three steps, expressed from forty different points of view, I hope to give you a sense of that journey towards fully human, soul-conscious living.

1

1. The Shell. Me. My body. My personality. My circumstances.
2. The Seed. The first gene, seed, saviour, word, archetype.
3. The Centre. The creator, unmanifest, source, space, heart.

2

1. My Personal body. Physical, emotional, astral, subtle body.
2. The Causal body. Seed body, human archetype.
3. No body. Nowhere is everywhere.

3

1. The body. Senses, mechanics of brain.
2. The soul. The essence of me.
3. The spirit. The essence of the All.

4

1. Many things. Mind all over the place. Nowhere.
2. One thing. Mind concentrated on one point. Right here.
3. No thing. One point expands into everything. Everywhere.

5

1. Conscious Mind. Above.
2. Subconscious Mind. Below.
3. Superconscious Mind. Everywhere.

6

1. Mind. The heavens.
2. Body. The earth.
3. Heart. The meeting place.

7

1. The out-breath. Losing all.
2. The in-breath. Gaining all.
3. The Divine breath. Sharing all.

8

1. The Inert. The gross, the material, the 'Tamasic'.
2. The Active. The intense, the passionate, the 'Rajasic'.
3. The Subtle. Ethereal, expansive, the 'Sattvic'.

9

1. Pleasure. Chasing pleasure, things, small horizons.
2. Pain. Disillusion, suffering, dashed dreams, struggle.
3. Bliss. The joy of being beyond pleasure and pain. Loving reality.

10

1. The child. I am the centre of the universe. Self centred.
2. The adult. I am separate, ego, alienated.
3. The child of God. The Universe created me. I belong.

11

1. I see.
2. I hear.
3. I feel.

12

1. Limited. I am trapped on the wheel.
2. Unlimited. I am free of the wheel.
3. Loving limitation. Helping the wheel move forward.

13

1. Whole.
2. Broken.
3. Wounded healer.

14

1. Speaking. Energy diffused. Words forgotten.
2. Silence. Energy concentrated. Suffused with presence.
3. The Word. Revelation. A few words, but with great impact.

15

1. Ease.
2. Struggle.
3. Purpose.

16

1. Doing without feeling.
2. Feeling without doing.
3. Doing with feeling.

17

Lost in the past.
Living in the present.
Igniting a brighter future.

18
1. Body. Identify with the body. Attachment.
2. Soul. Identify with the soul. Detachment.
3. Body and Soul. Body is soul in action. Love.

19
1. Without, God is without.
2. Within, God is within.
3. No within, no without.

20
1. Form. Lost in form.
2. Formlessness. Lost in formlessness.
3. Form is formless. Bringing quality into quantity.

21
1. Selfish. Cling to oneself. Foolish.
2. Selfless. Serve the other. Cling to Beloved. Loving.
3. Self is God. God is me. No difference. Wise.

22
1. Outer Guru. A personal relationship, personal training.
2. Inner Guru. The teachers' teacher. Mystical relationship.
3. Guru is everywhere. All are teachers and students.

23
1. Square. Safe, secure.
2. Triangle. Aspiring.
3. Circle. Complete.

24
1. Sakti. Lost in creation. The Mother. Endless expression.
2. Siva. Beyond creation. The formless. The creator. The Father.
3. Siva/Sakti. Eternal dance between creator and creation.

25
1. Birth – born into this world. I am matter.
2. Death – die to this world. I am spirit.
3. Rebirth – Spirit gives me new birth every day.

Transforming the battle of life into a dance

Crossing over the sea is an archetypal image of our journey into eternity

26

1. A boat. Staying afloat on the ocean. Ego.
2. The ocean. Letting go. Sinking. I am the ocean. Self.
3. A wave. Self expression through the Ego.

27

1. The ordinary. The routine.
2. The extra-ordinary. The amazing, spectacular.
3. The ordinary is extra-ordinary. Every moment is a miracle.

28

1.Flow. Life easy.
2 Blockage. Obstacles, difficulties. Contraction.
3 Breakthrough. New and better way forward. Expansion.

29

1. Conditioned. I must have things like this.
2. Unconditioned. I can have things any way.
3. Structured. To spread freedom, I use a structure.

30

1. No frame. I don't know where I'm going, what I'm for.
2. Frame. Working within this frame, I paint a picture.
3. Beyond the Frame. My picture speaks to many.

31

1. Undisciplined. Can't get it together.
2. Disciplined. I've got it together. I'm in control.
3. Spontaneous. I am a flute in the hands of my beloved.

32

1. No expression. I'm too afraid to dance or sing.
2. Self expression. I'm sung my song.
3. Revelation. The One is speaking through me.

33

1. Dreams and ideals.
2. Shattered dreams.
3. Reality breaking through, is so much more.

34

1. The left path – ease, satisfaction, pleasure, expression.
2. The right path – struggle, work, effort, restraint.
3. The middle way – the way of balance.

35

1. Full – no time, no space, busy,
2. Empty – all the time in the world, nothing to do.
3. Creative – making something from nothing.

36

1. World. Working to change the world.
2. Self. Working to change myself.
3. Self is the world. Changing myself, I change the world.

37

1. Outer goals. Achieving outer goals, within this lifetime.
2. Inner goals. Soul victories, that last many lifetimes.
3. Inner is Outer. Inner victory manifests in beautiful signs.

38

Dharana – concentrate on object.
Dhyana – meditate, flow with object.
Samadhi- realise, subject becomes object.

39

Truth – Become one.
Love – Give to the many.
Peace – All is complete.

40

Love yourself.
Love God.
Love.

BIBLIOGRAPHY AND NOTES

All the quotations above were sourced from the following publications.

Buddha

Dhammapada – The Sayings of the Buddha – Thomas Byrom – Shambala – Boston and London 1993.

Buddha – John Ortnor – Duncan Baird Publishers 2007

Teachings of the Buddha – Edited by Jack Kornfield – Shambala, Boston and London 1996

Rumi

Rumi – Whispers of the Beloved – Azima Melita Kolin and Maryam Mafi – Thorsons – 1999

The Love Poems of Rumi – Deepak Chopra – 1998 -Rider

Jesus

The Gospel of Jesus – St Paul Publications – 1979

Patanjali

Light on the Yoga Sutras of Patanjali – BKS Iyengar – Thorsons – 1996

Krishna

The Bhagavad Gita – Translation by Juan Mascaro - Penguin Classics – 1962

St Nicephorous of Mount Athos

On the Prayer of Jesus – Ignatius Brianchaninov – Element Books – 1987

St Symeon the New Theologian

The Philokalia – Faber and Faber – 1995

Guru Nanak

Sufis, Mystics and Yogis of India – Bankey Behari – Bharatiya Vidya Bhavan – 1982

Hafiz

I heard God Laughing – Daniel Ladinsky – Mobius Press – 1996

Lao Tzu

The Essential Tao – Thomas Cleary – Castle Books – 1998

The Sayings of Lao Tzu – Lionel Giles – Butler and Tanner – 1905

Svatmarama

The Hathayogapradipika of Svatmarama – The Adyar Library and Research Centre – 1972

Upanishads

The Upanishads – Eknath Easwaran – Arkana – Penguin – 1988

Baha'u'llah

Earth and air, water and fire – A personal approach to Spiritual Transformation – Arthur Weinberg